Suzy Gershman's

BORN TO SHOP

HONG KONG, SHANGHAI & BEIJING

The Ultimate Guide for Travelers Who Love to Shop

3rd Edition

WILEY

Wiley Publishing, Inc.

For the Hong Kong Home Team: Peter and Louisa, Glenn and Lucille, and Les Girls: Carole, Lynn, Sally, Sian, Susan, etc.

With thanks and love and double wishes for double happiness.

Published by:

Wiley Publishing, Inc.

111 River St.
Hoboken, NJ 07030-5774

ISBN 13: 978-0-7645-7864-9
ISBN 10: 0-7645-7864-2

Editor: Marie Morris
Production Editor: M. Faunette Johnston
Photo Editor: Richard Fox
Cartographer: Roberta Stockwell
Production by Wiley Indianapolis Composition Services

For information on our other products and services or to obtain technical support, please contact our Customer Care Department within the U.S. at 800/762-2974, outside the U.S. at 317/572-3993 or fax 317/572-4002.

Wiley also publishes its books in a variety of electronic formats. Some content that appears in print may not be available in electronic formats.

Manufactured in the United States of America

5 4 3 2 1

CONTENTS

MAP LIST

ABOUT THE AUTHORS

Suzy Gershman has been named "the world's greatest shopper" by amazon.com and "Super Shopper Suzy" by Oprah Winfrey. She has been a contributing editor—on the subject of international retail, of course—for *Travel + Leisure* and *National Geographic Traveler.* Gershman also writes for *Air-France Madame, Where Paris, Porthole,* and assorted other travel sources. She lives part-time in Paris, part-time in Provence, and part-time at the airport, but is looking for an apartment in Shanghai.

Aaron Gershman is a singer-songwriter living in Los Angeles, as well as contributing editor to *Born to Shop.* He writes on guys' fashions, boy toys, and electronics.

Jenny McCormick is a graduate student and part-time editorial assistant. She writes on fashion and trends for young women.

TO START WITH

Hong Kong has long been the door to the Orient. It's an important destination for those who will be visiting mainland China as well. Many go on to Bangkok; trendy travelers are keen on Cambodia and Laos. This edition of *Born to Shop* includes information about Hanoi and a new chapter on the Pearl River Delta that covers my first expedition into Canton, now known as Guangzhou. With the opening of the new railroad station in Kowloon, I have expanded the Shenzen coverage and added lodging information.

This edition has a lot more of Hong Kong in it than the previous one. And two twentysomethings have added their perspective—I have discovered that many generations of the same family are using my books.

Here's hoping you have as much shopping fun as we did, enjoy as many great family travels, and do not pay as much overweight.

Suzy Gershman
Paris, March 2005

Chapter One

....

THE BEST OF HONG KONG, SHANGHAI & BEIJING

May you live in interesting times. May you shop in somewhat dirty street markets. May you never pay more than 100 of anything (yuan, Hong Kong dollars, euros—whatever). May you get to China before it's too late. May you gaze into the new China and understand that you see the future, and it is powerful.

Hey, I know there's a real China out there. But as a visitor to Shanghai and Beijing, you will be hard pressed to find it. With the Olympics coming to Beijing in 2008, everything is getting cleaner and more generic. Hong Kong still shimmers as an oasis, although prices there are higher on most items (except designer goods, which cost 20% less than in mainland China).

Most visitors to Hong Kong stay only 3 or 4 days, then go on to another destination, such as mainland China or the Pacific Rim. On my latest adventure from Hong Kong, I dove into Macau, passed the Border Gate, zipped past Furniture Land (the space between Macao and Guangzhou, where antique furniture is born), and explored some of the Pearl River Delta cities. I did it for you and for the new China.

If you're antsy about the rate of exchange on the dollar against the euro, Asia is your new best friend. The rush is on—get going now. This chapter is a compilation of lists and suggestions to help guide you to the best, the brightest, and the most brilliant according to budget.

Please remember that coming up with a single best of anything is pretty hard. "Best" is a subjective thing. Each choice here is based on a combination of location, value, and energy.

Believe it or not, there isn't much crossover in merchandise in the cities this book covers; once you have left a destination, you may not have the luxury of another crack at a particular item.

Why didn't I buy more???

THE 10 BEST STORES

Along with my list comes the usual disclaimer—these choices are based on my research visits. China is changing fast. As soon as we go to press, a bigger or better resource might pop up. For the best stores in Hanoi, see p. 187. This list is in alphabetical order.

ASHNEIL
Far East Mansions, 5–6 Middle Rd., Shop 114 (up the stairs), Tsim Sha Tsui, Kowloon, Hong Kong (MTR: TST)

Calling this a store may lead you to believe it is bigger than a postage stamp, which it is not. More than two shoppers make it feel crowded. But that's only because it's piled high and deep with handbags of all sorts. They are not illegal fakes—they're excellent-quality items that look a good bit like styles you know and love but that have no phony parts (and, therefore, are not illegal). Prices begin at around $150 and go up (sometimes way up), but the bags are so well made that you often can't tell them from the $1,000 versions. You can have your purchases delivered to the U.S. (saving on the Customs allowance), order something made in a custom color, or buy small leather goods such as belts and wallets. Credit cards accepted.

BLANC DE CHINE
Pedder Building, 12 Pedder St., Room 201, Central, Hong Kong (MTR: Central)

Armani meets Shanghai Tang. Expect to pay $500 or more for a jacket, but the quality and the look will melt you.

CITY SUPER
Times Square mall (MTR: Causeway Bay); Ocean Terminal, Harbour City, Kowloon (MTR: TST); IFC2 mall (MTR: Central); all Hong Kong

As the name implies, this is a supermarket. The branches are not all equal—the one at Times Square is the best—but all are good enough to qualify for this list. You can buy Asian products (which make great gifts) as well as bath and beauty items and housewares.

HU & HU ANTIQUES
1685 Wuzhong Lu, Shanghai (no nearby Metro)

If you aren't interested in furniture, then you can skip this establishment. If you love to look at pretty things and adore high style with ultra panache, this is the most chic furniture store in all of China. The woman who runs it is American-Chinese and speaks English like few others in Shanghai. Aside from two warehouses filled with furniture, you'll find smaller items for your tabletop and to give as gifts. Have your taxi wait . . . even if it's for a few days.

LOTUS CENTRE
Super Brand Mall, Pudong, Shanghai (Metro: Lu Jia Zhui)

Lotus Centre is a chain, and I recommend any branch you can get to—this one is just easy for tourists. It is Kmart with a fancy supermarket: two floors of clothes and food and lifestyle and everything you want. Did I mention great prices?

MAYLIN

Peninsula Hotel Shopping Arcade, Salisbury Rd., Kowloon (MTR: TST), Hong Kong

The best Birkin in the biz. Expect to pay $300. Yes, U.S. But then, a Birkin costs around 10 grand, so don't whimper.

SHANGHAI TANG

Pedder Building, 12 Pedder St., Central, Hong Kong (MTR: Central)

This is undoubtedly one of the must-see, must-dos of Hong Kong, even if you don't buy anything. In fact, there is a good chance you *won't* buy anything. Still, the store is gorgeous to look at and inspirational in its creativity.

Shanghai Tang stocks souvenirs and fashions, Mao-mania, and original artwork by contemporary artists—all imported from China. Get a load of the gift wrap! Wander, drool, buy, have a cigar, sit down for tea, or shop 'til you're late for your next appointment.

SUCHOW COBBLER

3 Fuchow Rd., Shanghai

Don't sneeze or you will miss this tiny shop that specializes in a sophisticated twist on an old Chinese art—the embroidered slipper. About $50 a pair, but they look like a million.

X-QUISIT

Shop L141, Mall Place, InterContinental Hotel, Salisbury Rd. Kowloon, Hong Kong (MTR: TST)

The prices are high, but so is the level of imagination and style. The wide selection includes a variety of goods, from jewelry to robes, to housewares and gifts. Everything has an Asian twist without being costumey. The owner starred at Lane Crawford, the local department store, before going out on her own. This store is also a good inspiration for items that you can make yourself. On the other hand, several of the $600 necklaces aren't cost-effective as do-it-yourself pieces, so look, touch, and splurge.

Yue Hwa Chinese Products Emporium
301–309 Nathan Rd., Yau Ma Tei, Kowloon, Hong Kong (MTR: Jordan Rd.), and other locations

This department store comes complete with a grocery store in the basement. Buy every possible gift or souvenir, and don't forget the lower level for seal-penis wine or booze with snakes in it. This is where I found the best glitzy montage handbags—the style includes a photo process of an animal or old-timey poster, then heaps of sequins and doodads. They cost about $300 in U.S. department stores, $30 here.

Airports & You

Many businesspeople are in such a great hurry getting from meeting to meeting that they wait to shop at the airport duty-free shops as they're leaving town.

The **Hong Kong** airport may be a virtual shopping mall, but note that prices are not the same as in town. Even duty-free prices are high. I suggest hitting the gift shop at your hotel in Hong Kong if you're willing to pay top dollar. Gift shops will have slightly better prices and less pressure of the "Oh my, I'd better grab it" type.

The **Beijing** airport's duty-free shop is excellent for last-minute shopping. I can't tell you that the prices are the lowest in town, but the selection is wide enough for you to accomplish all your shopping goals.

Shanghai's Pudong Airport gift shops are even more sophisticated, in the TT (tourist trap) department. I've stocked up on chocolate-covered lichees and the most extraordinary embroidered satin bedroom slippers.

GREAT INEXPENSIVE GIFTS

- **Tea mugs.** Chinese tea mugs (complete with lid) cost about $3 each in any Chinese department store. You'll have to wrap them yourself (pack with care), but they make marvelous gifts.
- **Chinese tea.** From high-end brands and makers (such as Fook Ming Tong, in Hong Kong) to any old brand in a great-looking package sold on the street or at a Chinese department store, tea makes a very traditional gift, and it doesn't break. Prices vary with brand and venue.
- **"Jade."** I buy "jade" doughnuts by the dozen at the Jade Market in Hong Kong and then string each one individually as a gift. They cost about $1 each and are not real jade. If you're willing to pay $10 to $15 per gift, you can purchase animal figurines.
- **Chops.** You can be sure that no one else has one of these. A chop, or Chinese signature stamp, costs about $25 and can usually be carved while you wait.
- **Chopsticks.** I found the really chic ones—pearl inlay and all that—in Hanoi, not in China. They cost about $2 per pair.
- **Perfume bottles.** Many people like perfume bottles painted on the inside, but I prefer the fake antiques that look like smoked glass from the 1920s.

THE BEST SHOPPING EXPERIENCES

- Trolling for bargains on Fa Yuen Street, Hong Kong
- Having a garment made to measure in Hong Kong
- Any flea market in China
- Hanoi

BEST NEW SHOPPING CONCEPTS

••

In **Hong Kong,** you can soon shop at **Disneyland.** Although you can buy Disney souvenirs outside of the park, Disney has closed its freestanding stores in this area. At press time, the new park was scheduled to open in September 2005.

The big-name luxury hotels are fighting it out and opening in Hong Kong shopping malls. Located in office towers in Central, two of the biggest names offer shopping deals, packages, and perks. Check out the **Mandarin Landmark** in the Landmark and the **Four Seasons Hotel Hong Kong** in the IFC Tower.

In **Beijing,** shopping for Olympic souvenirs isn't new, but the official store is. Another innovation: The crackdown on fake Olympic merchandise—as well as designer fakes.

INSIDER CONCIERGE
InterContinental Hotel, Salisbury Rd., Tsim Sha Tsui, Hong Kong (MTR: TST)

Insider Concierge is an InterContinental trademark for a program under which the chain's super-duper concierges find you whatever you need. Actually, any good hotel concierge can provide this service, but InterConti backs this up with a fabulous team. And yes, the concierge can arrange for whatever you need to look at to be brought to your hotel room, or for fittings to be done in your room.

XINTIANDI
Huai Hai Rd. East, Shanghai (Metro: Huang Pi Nan Rd.)

Maybe it's not fair to call this an urban renewal effort—it's an entire city of renovated stone houses that have been turned into bars, restaurants, and shops with walkways in between and the most chic customers in all of China. You don't so much come here for the shopping as for the whole thing, usually at night, when the stores stay open late and you drink and stroll and then have dinner.

BEST WINDOW-SHOPPING CONCEPT

THREE ON THE BUND
No. 3 The Bund, 3 Zhong Shan Dong Yi Rd., at Guang-dong Rd. (Metro: Renmin Guangchang), Shanghai

I don't think we came to Shanghai to buy $400 Armani jeans, but this experience is still a thrill. Check out several floors of retail, then eat at one of the restaurants and plop down in the Evian spa. The whole shebang is so beautiful to look at that if you miss it, you are missing out.

THE BEST SOURCES FOR ANTIQUES

Antiques in China are tricky—you simply don't know what's real and what isn't. Hong Kong's Hollywood Road is an excellent stroll for antiques shopping, for getting an overview of what is available, and for learning what the prices might be. Don't buy anything serious from a dealer who is not known in the trade.

Macau is an excellent source for antiques. That is, if they weren't made right there!

Both Shanghai and Beijing abound with shopping ops for small decorative items and antiques, real and fake. Prices can be half those in Hong Kong. But then, reliability can be, too.

THE BEST MARKETS

DONG JIA DU FABRIC MARKET
Dong Jia Du Rd., Shanghai (no nearby Metro)

This is an enclosed market filled with stalls staggering under the weight of bolts of fabric. It also holds some tailor shops, and a few of the fabric shops sell ready-made garments or gift items. Fabric I saw for 86€ per meter at the fabric market in Paris was $15 here.

JADE MARKET
Kansu and Battery sts., Yau Ma Tei, Kowloon, Hong Kong (MTR: Jordan Rd.)

Two tents' worth of dealers with beads, jade, more jade, and a few antiques. Do-it-yourselfers will go wild. Check out Jenny Gems. To reach the market from the Metro, walk a bit or take a taxi.

PANJIAYUAN ANTIQUE AND CURIO MARKET/DIRT MARKET
Huaweiqiaxi Nan Dajie, Beijing (no nearby Metro)

If you are a flea market person, you owe it to yourself to arrange your trip so that you have a few hours here. Also known as the Dirt Market (it once had a dirt yard), the market includes some aisles of dealers under tin rooftops, and masses of real people with their goods laid out on the ground. Beware of fakes. The best time to shop is before 10am, when it gets very crowded. Open Saturday and Sunday only.

PEARL MARKET (HONG QIAO MARKET)
Near the Temple of Heaven, Beijing (no nearby Metro)

This indoor mall sounds a lot more romantic than it looks, but if you can adjust your expectations, you'll be on your way to heaven . . . and the Temple of Heaven is conveniently across the street.

The first floor has watches and small electronics (including Mao lighters), then there's leather goods and fakes. Also on this floor is luggage, which comes in handy when you run out of packing space and are desperate for cheap new bags. At the far end of this floor is a series of stalls selling Chinese arts and crafts and souvenir items. Next up is a floor of pearls and pearl wannabes, beads, gemstones, clasps, and beads. The rear of this floor holds a small mall of antiques shops.

THE BEST TAILORS

Prices in China for custom-made clothing may be less than in Hong Kong, but don't be tempted. If you want top-of-the-line quality that competes with the best of Savile Row, you want a Hong Kong tailor (whose family probably came from Shanghai anyway).

Hong Kong has no best tailor—it has two. They stand head and shoulders above the others for one simple reason: They have their own workrooms and do not send their piece-work to China. Only W. W. Chan & Sons has expanded to mainland China—it has a shop in Shanghai. Prices in Shanghai are approximately 20% less than in Hong Kong; the quality is the same.

A-MAN HING CHEONG CO. LTD.
Mandarin Oriental Hotel, 5 Connaught Rd., Hong Kong (MTR: Central)

W. W. CHAN & SONS LTD.
Burlington House, 92–94 Nathan Rd., 2nd floor, Kowloon, Hong Kong (MTR: TST); Shanghai Hilton Hotel, 250 Hua Shan Rd., Shanghai (Metro: Jing An Temple or Chang Shu Rd.); 129A-2 Mao Ming Rd., Shanghai (Metro: Shi Men Rd.)

BEST SHIRTMAKERS

All good tailors also make shirts, but two incredibly famous names in shirtmaking specialize in men's shirts, shorts, and pajamas only:

ASCOT CHANG CO. LTD.
The Peninsula Hotel, Salisbury Rd., Kowloon (MTR: TST); InterContinental Hotel, 18 Salisbury Rd., Kowloon (MTR: TST); Prince's Building, Chater Rd. (MTR: Central); all Hong Kong

DAVID'S SHIRTS
Victoria Hotel, Unit 201, Shun Tak Centre (MTR: Sheung Wan); Mandarin Oriental Hotel, 5 Connaught Rd. (MTR: Central); 33 Kimberley Rd., Kowloon (MTR: TST); all Hong Kong

My Five Best New Finds

by Suzy Gershman

- **Telephones:** Sure, I talk on the phone a lot, but I can't explain why I became obsessed with buying telephones in China—other than the colors and styles. The best ones I found recently were in street markets at East Gate in Shenzen, but I admit to drooling over the pink metallic plastic spaceship designs at **Lotus Centre** in Shanghai. Most phones cost $10.
- **Shinco DVD Player:** I thought Shinco was a no-name Chinese brand, but the Sony store near my apartment in Paris also sells it. So do Fortress and Broadway, the two reliable electronics chains in Hong Kong. My latest score is a portable DVD player the size of a CD player for $135. It's dual voltage (110–220), so I can travel with it and play DVDs on a TV set anywhere in the world.
- **Phone Fashion Accessories:** I can't stand it when my portable phone rings inside my handbag and I can't find it. Other people must have the same problem because most department stores around the world carry phone pouches. I found the most chic collection, made by Shanghai 1931, on sale in one of the gift shops in the lobby of the Okura Garden Hotel in Shanghai. They cost about $10 each and are made of Chinese silk with gorgeous knots at the corner. For information, contact the manufacturer (www.moonheart-hk.com).
- **Ancestors:** Paintings on canvas. I have been buying from the same dealer at the **Pearl Market** in Beijing. On the top floor, at the far end, away from the vendors who sell beads, pearls, and wannabe pearls, there's a small village of antiques

stands. Many of them sell scrolls with ancestors on them; I have bought all of mine here. I also got a canvas at the **Panjiayuan Antique and Curio Market** (also called the **Dirt Market**) in Beijing, and some scrolls at the flea market in Shanghai. Boy, have I got family now!

- **Chinese Shirts:** From Kenki, a small chain of arts and crafts clothing stores in Hong Kong, I bought reversible velvet-silk Chinese big shirts for $40.

My Best Finds

by Aaron James

- **DVDs:** Find 'em anywhere, for viewing pleasure, sure, but don't forget to read the packaging—really hilarious. Even if the DVDs don't work, they're worth the money just for the descriptions.
- **CDs:** In Shanghai you can find cheap and legal CDs in local stores—just weed through racks of Backstreet Boys and eventually you may find something decent.
- **Video Games:** I found Game Boy and other game system cartridges and cassettes in the Shanghai street market. Video games are cheap and contain several games on the same cassette. Of course, they may not be legal, and they may repeat the same game over and over.
- **Mao Bags:** Street vendors, especially in Shanghai, sell these. An over-the-shoulder Mao bag is a must for any young revolutionary.
- **Custom-Tailored Shirts:** In Shanghai I visited the showroom of W. W. Chan & Sons Ltd. (my father's tailor from Hong Kong) and was fitted for my first custom shirts. The quality of the shirts is unmatched. I was just measured for my first suit since my bar mitzvah ($650).

My Best Finds

by Jenny McCormick

- **Hair Sticks:** Plastic chopstick-style fashion statements that you poke into your hair—everything from faux tortoise shell to Burberry plaid. Talk 'em down to $1 each. Best selection: ground floor of the Pearl Market, Beijing.
- **Fake Jade "Doughnuts":** The Pearl Market and elsewhere, about $1.
- **Bamboo Handbag:** About $10 at the Dong Tai Market in Shanghai.
- **Mao Watch:** About $2. Available at most street markets but sold by the dozens at Hong Qiao and in the booths along Wangfujing, both in Beijing.
- **James Bond DVD Boxed Set:** For my dad. Bought in Shanghai—$25 for all 20 movies.

Chapter Two

....

ORIENTATION

As I look to August 2008, when Beijing plays host to the Olympics, I have two things to say:

- If you have any interest in seeing the old Beijing, or what existed of it into the early 21st century, get there now. Little of the old-fashioned charm will be left by 2008. In fact, in early 2005, most of old Beijing has disappeared.
- Hong Kong is far from over. Despite efforts to make Shanghai the new Hong Kong—which it will indeed be in perhaps 20 years—Hong Kong is fighting back most impressively. Everyone speaks English (a major plus), and the luxury hotels (Mandarin Landmark, Four Seasons) just keep coming, as do the big-name chefs.

THE MAGIC OF HONG KONG

....

The way I see it, Hong Kong will always be a little bit of heaven. It will remain the diamond in the crown for years to come simply because the locals speak English better than most residents of mainland China. They also understand customer service better, do luxury as it's never been done before, and offer shopping options in both European fit and Asian fit.

Sure, China's big cities offer plenty of European designer goods, but they cost 20% more than in Hong Kong, and they probably won't fit you. And the linen sheets at the Mandarin Oriental? The spa at the InterConti? Oh, my dear.

Hong Kong is still the gateway to China, and the best place to begin and finish any trip to the area.

THE NEW CHINA

This book covers the most obvious cities a tourist will visit, but I don't want you to think that Shanghai and Beijing are the only chic cities in China, that the new China is only along the east coast, or that there ain't a whole lot of shakin' goin' on. To make this clear, I'll list the cities where the Italian brand Max Mara has stores:

Beijing, Changchun, Chandu, Chongqing, Dalian, Guangzhou, Hangzhou, Harbin, Kunming, Qingdao, Shanghai, Shenyang, Shenzen, Urümqi, Wuhan, Xi'an.

Welcome to the new China; get out there and shop. Study a map, learn these cities, and book another ticket to come back.

WELCOME TO CHINA

I try to put politics aside when I write about China; after all, my mission is to shop. I can't help but note, however, that the Chinese are the most capitalist communists I've ever seen. They grasp the big picture and, my God, it's impressive.

Beijing and Shanghai are masterworks of marketing, in all senses and subtexts of the word. To market, to market, to score some fine buys. To market, to market, to influence the world. China is the future. Napoleon was right: When China awakes, the world will indeed tremble.

China

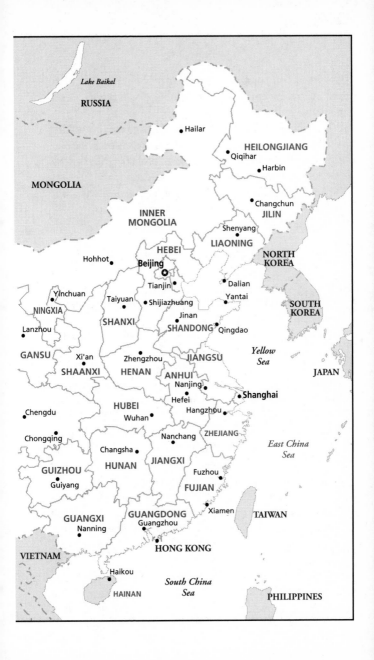

Getting a Visa

U.S. citizens do not need a visa to enter Hong Kong. They do need a visa to enter the People's Republic of China (PRC), even on a day trip from Hong Kong.

The Chinese make American and British passport holders pay a dear price for their visas. The most expensive is the one-year, multiple-entry visa, which a tourist probably will not need. A single-entry visa for a U.S. passport holder is HK$450 ($58). The waiting period for U.S. passport holders is 5 days. You can pay for rush service and get a visa in 24 hours.

There are a number of ways to get a visa:

- Apply for a visa through the Chinese consulate in your city.
- If you carry a secondary passport from a country other than the U.S. or U.K., use it to secure your Chinese visa. It will be much less expensive.
- If you are willing to pay the money or you live in a city that does not have a Chinese consulate, contact a visa service. Download the needed papers, fill them in, then send off your passport, one passport-size photo, and a big fat check by FedEx or another service that offers tracking. I use **Zierer Visa Service** (© **866/788-1100** or 212/265-7887; www.zvs.com); it charges about $50 in service fees (the price of the visa is additional), but you have to do very little. You are paying for convenience, and you will get your passport back, with hologram visa, in about a week. It is virtually impossible for a U.S. citizen to get a visa to enter China outside of the U.S. except through London, or in Hong Kong after you arrive. Zierer also has offices in London (Zierer Visa Service UK Ltd.; © **020-7833-2700**; www.visaservice.co.uk).
- Get your visa in Hong Kong. This can be pricey if you need fast service. There are visa services in the airport and throughout town, or your hotel concierge can get the visa. It's a cinch at the airport and costs about $135, but it takes

about 4 hours, which means hanging out at the airport or schlepping back and forth.

- For me, it was far easier to have my hotel concierge do all the work, though that's more expensive. When the concierge obtains your visa, your total bill is usually divided in two: the cost of the actual visa (about $150) and the service charge (about $50). You do not have to add a tip to a service charge.

Chinese Arrival Details

1. There is no limit on the amount of foreign cash you can legally bring into the PRC. However, if you have more than US$5,000, you must declare it.
2. No pornographic materials, guns, or bombs.
3. No live animals. Regulations on pets are being eased, however. The new Chinese chic is to walk your dog—but dogs are prohibited from most public spaces.

FLYING CONCEPTS

With the PRC opening up, demand has created more air routes into China. More and more airlines are fighting for hubs and for the loyalty of business and leisure travelers. The number of flights into China has doubled in the last 2 years. The type of craft flying long-haul routes is also changing. Airlines are working to make the trip more comfortable with the addition of a new class of service—executive economy—and longer flying times. Yep, you can now fly nonstop from New York to Hong Kong in slightly over 15 hours.

The destination chapters that follow include specific tips on flights, carriers, and savings. Below are some concepts that will help you organize your trip.

If you are planning on exploring a little of China or looking for promotional deals, don't forget to check out the international airports of the Pearl River Delta, which include the brand-new Baiyun International Airport in Guangzhou.

Big Announcement

For those of you who will book all or part of your trip through Beijing, be aware that most airlines refer to Beijing as Pekin: This is the city's official airline designation. When checking flights listed in alphabetical order, look under *P* for Pekin. I even had trouble getting tickets to Beijing when the agent told me that the carrier served only Shanghai and Pekin in China, and I had to choose one.

Transpacific Flying

Many flights from the major West Coast cities (Los Angeles, San Francisco, Seattle, and Vancouver) connect through Narita or even Seoul. You may not enjoy the layovers.

Travelers increasingly prefer transpacific nonstops, with flying times of 13 to 16 hours. The longest flight these days is New York to Singapore on a transpacific route, some 18 hours of flying time, with **Singapore Airlines.**

Continental Airlines (www.continental.com) flies nonstop from Newark Liberty International Airport. Its business-first-class offers a first-class experience at a business-class price.

Cathay Pacific also flies a transpacific route from New York.

From the South or Midwest, you may want to travel through the major West Coast gateway cities (listed above).

I like **Northwest** for several reasons, including the possibility of a layover in Minneapolis, not far from the Mall of America. What a way to fight jet lag! Northwest also uses its Detroit hub for flights to China—it's less crowded than other U.S. international airports, and a secret worth remembering.

Don't forget to look into **Eva Air** (www.evaair.com), which flies the Taiwan flag. It offers service from major cities around the world and is known for the excellent luxury-coach section of the plane.

Finally, see specifics of travel to each destination in this book in subsequent chapters.

Transatlantic Routes

For the transatlantic approach, you can get to Hong Kong or the PRC from a variety of European hubs with ongoing flights to Asia. When I lived on the East Coast of the United States, I found it much easier to fly to London or Zurich, lay over for the weekend, beat the first 6 hours of jet lag (and go shopping), and then fly to Asia. The next 6 hours of jet lag were a lot easier to handle. Also note that **Lufthansa** operates 60 flights a week to Asia, so you may get more options on a transatlantic route. **KLM,** which code-shares with Delta and Air France, has flights from Amsterdam for about $750 in class H.

Competition on U.K.-to-China routes is fierce, so deals abound. **Virgin Atlantic** flies to Hong Kong and Shanghai; it has four classes of service, and double beds on long-haul flights. British Air and Cathay Pacific also fly from London. All match each other's promotional deals. I've heard of round-trips from London for $300.

When you are departing China, be sure to show your through ticket to the U.S. even if you are laying over in a European destination. If you have a ticket to the U.S., the U.S. luggage allowance, which is less rigid than the European one, will apply.

The transatlantic approach from the U.S. makes sense only if you take the time to lay over for at least 1 night.

Unusual Connections

- **Hawaii:** Service from Hawaii to Hong Kong is available, as is service on to China. This means that those who want to break up the flight, and avoid Narita, can stop over in Hawaii.
- **Tel Aviv:** This route is unusual, but it works. El Al uses Tel Aviv as the hub city and has ongoing service to Beijing and

Hong Kong as well as other major cities in the Far East. It's not as strange as it sounds—the flying time from New York to Tel Aviv is about the same as New York to Tokyo. A layover in Israel goes a long way toward eliminating jet lag once you get to China. Furthermore, El Al has a code share with American Airlines, so you can use frequent-flier miles, book through American, or perhaps connect an around-the-world deal with American, El Al, and Cathay Pacific.

• **Detroit:** This U.S. hub is not as well known as Chicago, so you have a better chance of using frequent-flier miles for the ticket. Northwest Airlines flies from Detroit to Guangzhou.

Flying on Miles

While you may indeed be able to use frequent-flier miles for your ticket to Asia, do check if the routing is worth it. My friend Mary had to fly West Palm Beach to Atlanta, Atlanta to L.A., L.A. to Seoul, and Seoul to Hong Kong. On one of her other trips, she had a 6-hour layover in Tokyo before the 5-hour flight to Hong Kong. In booking the trip, she was able to get only certain legs in business or first class and had to endure portions of her 30-hour journey in an economy seat.

Ticket Deals

Because they buy in bulk, wholesalers often get a better price. Enter **Lillian Fong,** my personal secret weapon in the U.S., and **Chen Voyages,** my French connection.

I have been using Lillian for over 20 years; I swear by her. Contact her at Pacific Place, 288 W. Valley Blvd., Suite 206B, Alhambra, CA 91801 (© **626/943-1212;** pacplace@att.net.com).

If you want to travel through Paris (or any other European city) or want to pay your fare in euros, try Chen Voyages, 137 rue de Tolbiac, 75013 Paris France (© **011-33-1-45-70-76-08;** www.chenvoyages.com). The staff speaks English fluently, and the company offers excellent deals.

Other thoughts:

- Talk to your travel agent about coupons or deals that can upgrade you to first class. Lillian once offered me first-class upgrade tickets if I paid the full fare for business class; that's a pretty good deal. The deals come and go with the seasons and the world situation. Note that travel to the area is up, so deals are not as easy to come by as they once were.
- There are so many code shares these days that you can have seamless ticketing; however, you may want to know which carriers are taking you on which legs.
- Do look for new carriers, new routes, and new connections that might offer promotional deals. Eva Air, a Taipei airline, is only a few years old but has gotten a lot of attention.
- Airlines often wage "mile wars"; recently you could fly to Hong Kong (coach) for 40,000 miles on a promotional deal.
- As the PRC opens up and technology allows airliners to fly farther, possibilities multiply. Watch for flights like Detroit–Shanghai, Minneapolis–Beijing, Houston–Taipei, and so on.
- Look for flights into unfamiliar Chinese cities, such as Shenzen or Guangzhou (Canton), both of which are near Hong Kong but in the PRC.
- Hunt down little-known promotional deals. For example, if you hold an American Express platinum card, you qualify for a free ticket to any destination when you buy a full-fare business-class ticket for yourself.
- Online fares may offer deals. Cathay Pacific's CyberTraveler (www.cathay-usa.com) provides e-mail updates about contests, deals, and even auctions.
- Check if the airline will let you buy a coach seat and a confirmed upgrade at the same time. To get a deal on these, you have to fly on certain days of the week and may not get the upgrade in both directions.
- Use your miles to upgrade, but only if the upgrade can be confirmed.

- Around-the-world fares may offer you the best price, especially in business and first class. They are also said to be more forgiving on jet lag because your body is always going in the same direction. Fares vary with the airline and the point of departure.
- A multiple-city trip around the Far East can be a great deal. Cathay Pacific's All Asia Pass costs less if you buy it through the website. *Also note:* A pass may not earn mileage points.
- Check out age-related discounts. Cathay Pacific considers you a senior citizen at age 55, and you get a $100 discount. Also investigate breaks for students and children.

Tours to China

Tours seem to be easy to find through travel agents and airline packages. I happened on an ad for a firm called Pacific Bestour, with such incredible prices that I was really impressed. The tours included airfare on United from the West Coast of the U.S. (other cities are available), transportation within China, daily breakfast, some city tours, an English-speaking guide, and more. Beijing tours began at $729; Hong Kong was $699. There was a 9-day tour that included Beijing and an Eastern Yangtze cruise for $999.

Chinese Carriers

AirChina (www.airchina.com.cn) is the best-known Chinese airline; it has code shares with a variety of well-known airlines and flies some 260 routes within China and over 50 international routes.

Other brands to know about—especially for domestic flights in China—include **China Eastern** (www.ce-air.com) and **China Southern** (www.cs-air.com). China Southern also serves international routes.

Cathay Pacific (www.cathaypacific.com) flies the Hong Kong flag and is part owner of Dragonair (www.dragonair.com), the best of the short-haul carriers from Hong Kong into China.

All About Eva

Eva Airways (www.evaair.com) is a Taiwanese carrier that flies to Hong Kong, Taipei, and various Southeast Asian and Australian destinations on brand-new planes (777s). Fares are excellent. If you buy a promotional business-class ticket (the best deals are available online), it's less than $2,000 round-trip. Executive coach goes for about $1,000. U.S. cities served include Los Angeles, San Francisco, Seattle, and Newark. Eva also flies from Paris.

This airline comes highly recommended by my travel agent Lillian Fong; I plan on testing it soon.

SLEEPING MATTERS

Each city chapter of this book includes specifics on hotels in the area. As China opens up, more and more hotels want part of the action. Where there are openings, there are promotional deals. **W Hotels,** a division of Starwood, plans to open in Hong Kong (West Kowloon) and in Shanghai (Pudong). The hotels will have W Retail, the store that sells objects from the rooms themselves.

Note also the trend for big hotel chains to open two hotels in the same city. **InterContinental** is currently building two hotels in Beijing—on opposite sides of the city. When you book any hotel, especially when there may be multiples, be sure you know which is where.

If you are interested in discounts, check out **www.asia-hotels.com**. Hey, you never know.

Websites for the major hotel chains with hotels in Hong Kong and the main cities in China:

- www.accorhotels.com/asia
- www.fourseasons.com

- www.hilton.com
- www.hyatt.com
- www.interconti.com (includes InterContinental and Holiday Inn)
- www.mandarinoriental.com
- www.peninsula.com
- www.starwood.com (includes Sheraton, St. Regis, Westin, and W Hotels)

MONEY MATTERS

The major currencies in this part of the world are:

- Hong Kong dollars, represented by HK$ preceding the amount
- Chinese yuan, often represented by a ¥ symbol following the amount. Yuan are also called RMB.
- Patacas, used in Macau and written MP$.

Note that most vendors in Vietnam prefer U.S. dollars. See p. 178 for more on financial matters in Hanoi. The Chinese yuan is not floated internationally, but at press time, the Chinese government revalued the currency and announced that it would no longer be pegged to the U.S. dollar. The effect on prices of consumer goods remains to be seen.

Money Tips

Having watched the fall of the dollar over the past few years, I can't begin to stress how important it is to shop in foreign destinations that are not affected by the rise of the euro. Well, it's important if you care about price.

So just being in Asia and shopping smart is **Tip #1.**

Tip #2: In major cities in eastern China, you can use Hong Kong dollars, but they are usually accepted at par. In reality, they are 10% more valuable, so you are losing money but gaining convenience. Your call.

Tip #3: If you visit Hong Kong before heading into the PRC, most major banks' ATMs will allow you to withdraw Chinese yuan, which appear on the screen as RMB. That means you won't have a money crisis as soon as you land or cross the border.

Currency Rates

Keep in mind that when you change money in hotels, you get the rate the hotel wants to give you, not the bank rate.

Note: At press time, the Chinese government revalued the currency and announced that the yuan would no longer be pegged to the U.S. dollar. For the most current exchange rates, go to www.oanda.com or www.xe.com.

One **U.S. dollar** is approximately equal to 7.7 Hong Kong dollars or 8.2 Chinese yuan.

One **euro** is approximately equal to 10 Chinese yuan or Hong Kong dollars.

One **pound sterling** is equal to approximately 14 Chinese yuan or Hong Kong dollars.

Note that the exchange rate varies widely depending on where you exchange your money; hotels and currency exchange offices often have the worst rates.

Charge It, Please

Credit cards are more and more widely accepted in China but are not as popular in Vietnam. That doesn't mean you can use your card with wild abandon in the PRC, however. In fact, you will find it easier to bargain and to pay in cash.

ATMs are all over China and Hong Kong, so you can get cash relatively easily. Be aware, however, that your bank may charge a high fee for international withdrawals.

About Those Tips

In mainland China, a communist country, tipping is frowned upon. A few hotels specifically ask you not to tip. But wait, if those people are communists, then I am Janus, the god with two faces. (That was Janus, wasn't it?) Some Chinese travel agencies now suggest that their clients tip guides 10% each day. Ha! Seems like anything goes.

I think tipping helps to teach capitalism. You can tip in U.S. dollars or euros in all of these countries. If I were you, I'd sit on the euros—they're more expensive for you and less convenient for the recipient.

Final Money Note

Prices given in this book are in U.S. dollars unless otherwise specified.

PHONING HOME

The least expensive way to phone home from Asia is with a phone card. Yes, you have to dial a lot of numbers, but you can talk for an hour for about $10. You can usually buy one from your hotel concierge, and they're available at any convenience store in Hong Kong or China, such as 7-Eleven. Access numbers for **AT&T** users:

Hong Kong: 800-96-1111 or 800-93-2266
Beijing: 108-888
Shanghai: 108-11

COMPARISON SHOPPING

People often ask me what city has the best deals or what to buy where in order to save money. There is no clear answer to that question. In terms of merchandise, I find different things in each city, without much cross-over. To confuse you more, I am borrowing part of a chart I found in *The Wall Street Journal Asia* that compared prices for a 700mL bottle of Chivas Regal. Prices have been translated into U.S. dollars.

Shanghai $25.40
Hong Kong $42.06

Who would have thunk it?

As a rule of thumb, China is less expensive than Hong Kong on basics and more expensive on designer goods and imports. Prices for Hong Kong designer goods are competitive with prices in Europe, but if you have to trade for euros, you are sunk—so Hong Kong might offer a bargain when compared to a European branch of the same designer store. The U.S. branch may still be less expensive.

THE WHOLE SHEBANG

As you organize your tour of Hong Kong, the PRC, and the Pacific Rim, perhaps you'll be interested in a recent survey from the Pacific Area Travel Association. Of the 39 official destinations in the area, the top 15 destinations in order of tourist entries are: Cambodia, Macau, Mongolia, Taiwan, Laos, Malaysia, Myanmar, Singapore, Maldives, Thailand, Guam, China, Hong Kong, Viet Nam, and the Cook Islands. You can get to all of these places from Hong Kong.

Chapter Three

....

A DICTIONARY OF CHINESE CRAFTS, STYLE & CUSTOMS

AN ALPHABETICAL GUIDE

....

Ancestor Paintings

Available on paper scroll or canvas scroll, these large paintings, most often family portraits, are called "ancestor paintings" in English and represent a very specific art form. They are widely copied and reproduced, so fakes abound. The best one I ever saw was of two female twins. My guide that day translated the inscription—about what venerable old ladies they were in that, their 42nd year on Earth.

Genuine antique paintings on canvas bought in China cost $500 to $3,000 each, depending on size and condition. Fake ancestors abound. I recently bought two beauties; the canvas was original but had been painted over. Although this totally ruins the investment or resale value, it made for two glorious wall hangings.

Antiques

Ha! I've seen antiques being made right in front of my eyes, and if I can't tell the difference, you can't, either. Be an expert, use an expert, or go to a trusted gallery.

The U.S. government defines an antique as any item of art, furniture, or craft work over 100 years old. If you return to the States with a genuine antique, you pay no duty on the piece.

True antiques are a hot commodity, and unscrupulous dealers take advantage of the demand by issuing authenticity papers for goods that are not old. To make matters worse, Hong Kong does not require its dealers to put prices on their merchandise. Depending on the dealer's mood or assessment of your pocketbook, he might quote you a price of HK$100 ($13) or HK$1,155 ($150) for the ginger jar you love. He also might tell you it's 10 years old or 10,000. If 1,000-year-old eggs, sold in all markets, aren't really 1,000 years old, imagine how that translates to antiques.

Pick a reputable dealer, and ask a lot of questions about the piece and its period. If the dealer doesn't know and doesn't offer to find out, he probably is not a true antiques expert. Get as much in writing as possible. Even if it means nothing, it is proof that you have been defrauded if you find out later that your Ming vase was made in Kowloon around 1995.

Your invoice should state what you are buying, the estimated age of the item (including dynasty and year), where it was made, and any flaws in or repairs done to the piece.

In good shops, the dealers want to tell you everything they know about a piece or a style you have expressed interest in; they're dying to talk about the items and to educate you. They take pleasure in talking about and explaining the ins and outs of entire categories of goods. If a dealer does not readily offer these free lessons, walk out.

Expect most, or many, of the antiques in markets in Hong Kong, Macau, and mainland China to be fakes.

Blue-and-White

Blue-and-white is the common term for Chinese export-style porcelain, which reached its heyday in the late 17th century, when the black ships were running "china" to Europe as if it were gold. After 1750, craftspeople in both England and continental Europe had the secret of bone china and were well on their way to creating their own chinoiserie styles and manufacturing transfer patterns for mass use.

The untrained eye needs to look for the following: pits and holes that indicate firing methods, the nonuniform look of hand drawing versus stencils, the shades of blues of the best dyes, and the right shades of gray-white as opposed to the bright white backgrounds of new wares. Marks on the bottom are usually meaningless. Designs may have European inspiration (look for flowers and arabesques), which will help you determine what you are looking at.

Bound Feet

Because a woman's place was in the home and women were to be kept barefoot and pregnant, the feet of aristocratic women were bound during infancy so that the women could not walk—meaning they had to be carried, were most comfortable prone, and certainly couldn't work.

The binding process brought the toes underneath the foot toward the heel and resulted in a permanently deformed foot. Special shoes were needed; they are still available in flea markets and are highly collectible. Watch out for reproductions, however.

Bronzes

Several Hong Kong museums feature antique Chinese bronzes, making the art form an easy one with which to commence your education in Chinese art. Visit several local museums to sharpen your eye; you'll want to understand the difference between what will cost you thousands of dollars and what you can buy for a few hundred. The lesser price indicates a fake. As with all Chinese art, you must be able to recognize subtle changes in style and form that indicate time periods and dynasties in order to properly date your fake.

Carpets

Carpets come in traditional designs or can be special-ordered at factories. Price depends on knots per square inch, fiber content, complexity of design, the number of colors used, and the city or region of origin. Any of the **Chinese Arts & Crafts** stores is a good place to look at carpets and get familiar with different styles and price ranges. You can visit the **Tai Ping Carpets** showroom in Hong Kong; many mainland tours include visits to carpet factories. Of course, your guide gets a kickback—what a silly question!

When considering the material of the rug, consider its use. Silk rugs are magnificent and impractical. If you're going to use the carpet in a low-traffic area or as a wall hanging, great. Silk threads are usually woven as the warp (vertical) threads, with either silk or cotton as the weft (horizontal). The pile in either case will be pure silk. Wool rugs are more durable.

I once bought fabulous needlepoint carpets at the Friendship Store in Beijing. Needlepoint carpets are now hard to find in China; I haven't seen any in about 5 years. But I often spot them in the United States at TJ Maxx. Go figure.

Ceramics & Porcelain

Ceramic and porcelain wares available in Hong Kong and China fall into three categories: British imports, new Chinese, and old Chinese. For a short lesson in buying blue-and-white, see above.

New Chinese craft pottery and porcelain is in high demand. Although much of the base material is being imported from Japan and finished in Hong Kong, it is still considered Chinese. In fact, the better wares are coming out of Hong Kong, and the mass-market stuff is more likely to come from China. Most factories will take orders directly. Numerous factories in Hong Kong will allow you to watch porcelain wares being created and to place a personal order.

Porcelain is distinguished from pottery, in that it uses china clay to form the paste. Modern designs are less elaborate than those used during the height of porcelain design in the Ming dynasty (A.D. 1368–1644), but the old techniques are slowly being revived. Blue-and-white ware is still the most popular. New wares (made to look old) can be found at various Chinese government stores, including **Chinese Arts & Crafts,** in zillions of little shops on and off Hollywood Road in Hong Kong, in Hong Kong's **Stanley Market,** in Macau, and just about everywhere else. Fakes abound; buy with care. When you order ceramics or ceramic lamps, you may even be asked whether you want "antique finish."

Cheongsam

You already know what a cheongsam is; you just don't know the word, so you're temporarily thrown. Close your eyes and picture Suzie Wong. She's wearing a Chinese dress with Mandarin collar and silk knot buttons that run from the neck across the shoulder and then down the side, right? Possibly in red satin with a dragon print, but that's an extra. The dress style is called a cheongsam. Really touristy ones come in those silk or satin looks, but you can buy a chic one or you can have one custom-made. In Shanghai, a cheongsam may be called a *quipo*.

Chinese New Year

During the Chinese or lunar new year, most stores close. For a few days preceding the festivities, it is not unusual for local retailers to raise prices: Shopkeepers take advantage of the fact that the Chinese like to buy new clothing for the new year.

Chinese Scrolls

Part art and part communication, Chinese scrolls are decorative pieces of parchment paper rolled around pieces of wood at each end. They contain calligraphy and art relating to history, a story, a poem, a lesson, or a message. Some scrolls are mostly art, with little calligraphy; others are just the opposite.

It is usually not possible to identify the author or artist, but doing so makes the scroll more valuable. Chinese scrolls make beautiful wall hangings and are popular collector's pieces.

Chinoiserie

Exports from Asia were so fashionable in Europe in the late 18th century, and again in the Victorian era, that they started their own trend. Western designers and craftspeople began to make items in the style of Asia. Much was created from fantasy and whimsy; the influence of Indian and other styles mixed with the purely Chinese. Decorative arts and furniture in Asian style, made in Europe, are considered chinoiserie. Chinoiserie is not actually made in China.

Chops

A chop is a form of signature stamp on which the symbol for a person's name is carved. The chop is then dipped in dry dye and placed on paper, much like a rubber stamp. The main difference between rubber stamps and chops is that rubber stamps became trendy only in the 20th century, whereas chops were in vogue about 2,200 years ago. Because chops go so far back, you can choose from an antique or a newly created version.

Cloisonné

The art of cloisonné involves fitting decorative enamel between thin metal strips on a metal surface. The surface is then fired at just the right temperature, and the finish is glazed to a sheen. It sounds simple, but the work involved in laying the metal strips to form a complicated design and then laying in the paint so that it does not run is time consuming and delicate. It is an art requiring training and patience.

Antique works by the finest artists bring in large sums of money. Most of what you'll see for sale in Hong Kong (outside of the finest galleries) is mass-produced cloisonné and is inexpensive—a small vase sells for about $20; bangle bracelets are $3. You can also find rings, mirrors, and earrings for good prices at most markets. These make good souvenir gifts. Frankly, I prefer the Hermès version.

Embroidery

The art of stitching decorations onto fabric is known as embroidery. Stitches can be combined to make abstract or realistic shapes, sometimes of enormous complexity. Embroidered goods sold in Hong Kong include a variety of items: bed linens, chair cushions, tablecloths, napkins, runners, place mats, coasters, blouses, children's clothing, and robes. All of those items are new. There is another market in antique embroidered fabrics (and slippers), which is, of course, a whole different price category. Antique embroidery items can be very expensive.

Traditionally, embroidery was hand-sewn. Today machines do most of the work. Embroidery threads range from the finest silk to the heaviest yarn. Judge the value of a piece by whether it is hand-stitched or machine-stitched and by the kind of thread or yarn.

Fakes

China has seriously cracked down on makers of fake name-brand goods. Officials mostly go after the factories that produce the goods, so vendors still have the items, which they sell when conditions appear to be safe. Buying a fake doesn't make you safe, however—many are confiscated when you leave the area or when you enter the U.S. (and EU countries, too). I tried mailing DVDs to France and to the States, and in both cases, the packages never arrived.

Freebr

Pronounced "V-bra" or "Free-bra," this is a trademark of a company in Singapore that makes a brassiere without a back that sticks to your bosom. It's made of two gel forms—available in pinky flesh tone or gray—and the branded version in its hot pink box costs about $20. The notion is so popular that no-name copies are available in many street markets. You can buy according to cup size (B or C). Market versions cost about half as much as the branded ones, depending on your bargaining skills.

Furniture

Chinese styles in furniture once caused a major sensation in the European market. Teak and ebony were imported from the Far East and highly valued in the West. Yet the major furnishing rage was for lacquered goods, usually in the form of small chests of cabinets. The cabinets sat on top of stands, which were built to measure in Europe.

True Chinese antique furniture is defined by purity of form, with decorative and interpretive patterns carved into the sides or backs.

Antique furniture is a hot collector's item. Dealers and collectors alike scour the shops and auction houses. It is better to find an unfinished piece and oversee its restoration than to find one that has already been restored. If it has been restored, find out who did the work and what was done. Some unknowing dealers bleach the fine woods and ruin their value. Others put a polyurethanelike gloss on the pieces and make them unnaturally shiny.

Because Asian furniture is used to the local climate, be certain that your hometown weather will not damage the furniture you buy and that you have the proper humidifiers. Many shoppers say it's better to buy furniture from cities farther south in China and Asia, and not to buy in Beijing.

If you decide to buy, decide beforehand how you will get the piece home. If you are having the shop ship it, verify the quality of the shipper and insurance. If you are shipping it yourself, call a shipper and get details before you begin to negotiate the price of the piece. Ask about duty. I once paid $250 for a small piece and ended up paying an additional $425 to get it to my door—the shipping wasn't very expensive, but the duty was.

Horn

Tortoise shell is illegal to buy and import into the U.S., but most Asian tortoisey-looking items are made out of buffalo horn. Ask.

Ivory

One word of warning: Articles made from raw ivory will not be allowed into the United States. Only antique pieces made from carved ivory are allowed in, and only if the dealer provides the proper paperwork and provenance. It is not smart to try to run raw ivory. It's risky on several levels, so you may want to forget this category of goods.

Another word of warning: New items that look like ivory are made of other materials, including walrus bone and even nut. Carvers in Hong Kong are currently using dentin from walruses, hippopotamuses, boars, and whales as substitutes for elephant ivory. If you want to make sure you are not buying elephant ivory, look for a network of fine lines that is visible to the naked eye. If the piece you are buying is made of bone, it will not have any visible grain or luster. Bone also weighs less than ivory. Imitation ivory is made of plastic but can be colored to look quite good. However, it is a softer material and less dense than real ivory.

Jade

The term *jade* is used to signify two different stones: jadeite and nephrite. The written character for jade signifies purity, nobility, and beauty. Some consider it a magical stone, protecting the health of the person who wears it. The scholar always carried a piece of jade in his pocket for health and wisdom. Jade is also reported to pull impurities out of the body; old, red-brown jade reputedly has absorbed the blood and impurities of its deceased former owner.

Jadeite is chemically different from nephrite and tends to be more translucent. For this reason, jadeite is often considered to be more valuable. Furthermore, really good jade—sometimes called "imperial jade"—is white, not green.

In Chinese, *chen yu* is real jade, and *fu yu* is false jade. Jadeite comes in many colors, including lavender, yellow, black, orange, red, pink, white, and many shades of green. Nephrite comes in varying shades of green only.

The value of both is determined by translucence, quality of carving, and color. Assume that an inexpensive carving is not jade. "Jade" factories work in soapstone or other less valuable stones. Poor-quality white jade can be dyed into valuable-looking shades of green. Let the buyer beware.

Jade should be ice-cold to the touch and so hard it cannot be scratched by steel. Some shoppers make it common practice to quick-touch or lick-touch a piece. This is not a real test of good jade, although stone will certainly feel different to the tongue than plastic. You may also want to "ring" a piece, because jade, just like fine crystal, has its own tone when struck.

If you are interested in carved jade figures, bring out your own jeweler's loupe and watch the dealer quake. If the carving is smooth and uniform, it was done with modern tools. Gotcha! A fine piece and an old piece are hand-cut and should be slightly jagged on the edges.

What are those green circles you see in the market and often in the street? They are nephrite and should cost no more than $1 per circle. These "jade doughnuts" make fabulous gifts when tied to a long silken cord and turned into a necklace.

Kites

On one of my trips to China, I bought two very similar kites: One cost $26 in a hotel gift shop, and one cost $2 in Tiananmen Square. If you are buying the kite for a child who will most likely destroy it, get smart.

It is believed that kites first appeared about 2,400 years ago, first made of wood and bamboo and later refined in silk or paper, which had better draft. While kite flying is a hobby and an entertainment, it is also a science based on aeronautical engineering. In fact, early kites were used for military purposes, but around the year 784 and the start of the Tang dynasty, people began to fly kites for entertainment.

Among the most common folk motifs in kites are dragons and bats—bats being a figure for good luck, based on a pun with the Chinese word *fu,* which means "bat" and "blessing."

The value of a kite depends on the construction of the frame, the fabric, and the artistic merit of the designs.

Lacquer

No, I don't mean nail varnish. I'm talking about an ancient art form dating as far back as 85 B.C. Baskets, boxes, cups, bowls, and jars are coated with up to 30 layers of lacquer in order to make them waterproof. Each layer must be dried thoroughly and polished before another layer can be applied. After the lacquer is finished, decoration may be applied. Black (on the outside) and red (on the inside) is the most common color combination.

You may date an item by the colors used; metallics in the decorative painting were used by the Han dynasty. Modern (post-1650) versions of lacquer may be European-inspired chinoiserie; beware.

Lanterns

Several styles of lanterns are for sale in Hong Kong and China. Because they have become a fashion statement in home style lately, reproduction lanterns abound. Antique lanterns are available in some markets in Beijing and Shanghai; they are most often made from wire with red fabric inserts. Plastic lanterns are popular in Hong Kong during the Mid-Autumn Festival and are sold on the street for the night parades.

Monochromatic Wares

You may adore blue-and-white porcelain, but remember that it was created for export because locals thought it was ugly. The good stuff was usually monochromatic. Go to a museum and study the best and brightest before you start shopping because fakes abound.

Celadon is perhaps the best known of the Chinese porcelain monochromes. It is pale gray-green and gained popularity because of the (false) assumption that poisoned food would cause a piece of celadon pottery to change color. The amount of iron in the glaze determines the amount of green in the piece.

Mooncakes

Just as Anglo-Saxons associate Christmas with fruitcake, the Chinese give mooncakes for the Mid-Autumn Festival. The mooncake is the food that inspired Americans to invent the fortune cookie. It dates to a successful revolt against Mongol warlords. The Chinese communicated with messages that were baked into the little cakes. Now the cakes are a form of celebration, and design and packaging become a big part of the shopping process and the price. More than 30 brands are sold in Hong Kong; one large department store sells 10,000 mooncakes a day. There are several types—with lotus flour, with bean paste, and even with a hard-boiled duck egg as the prize in the center.

Opals

Hong Kong is the opal-cutting capital of Asia. Dealers buy opals, which are mined mainly in Australia, in their rough state and bring them to their factories in Hong Kong. There they are judged for quality and cut either for wholesale export or for local jewelry. Black opals are the rarest and most expensive. White opals are the most available; they are not actually white, but varying shades of sparkling color.

The opal has minuscule spheres of cristobalite layered inside; this causes the light to refract and the gem to look iridescent. The more cristobalite, the more "fire." An opal can contain up to 30% water, which makes it very difficult to cut. Dishonest dealers will sell sliced stones, called doublets or triplets, depending upon the number of slices of stone layered together. If the salesperson will not show you the back of the stone, suspect that it is layered.

Paper Cuts

An art form still practiced in China, paper cuts are hand-painted and hand-cut drawings of butterflies, animals, birds, flowers, and human figures. Often they are mounted on cards; sometimes they are sold in packs of six, delicately wrapped in tissue. We buy them in quantity and use them as decorations on cards and stationery.

Pearls

Pearls have been appreciated and all but worshipped in Eastern and Western cultures for centuries. Numerous famous women in history have had enviable pearl collections. They include Queen Elizabeth I, Queen Elizabeth II, Elizabeth Taylor, Coco Chanel, and Barbara Hutton, whose pearls were once owned by Marie Antoinette.

The first thing to know about shopping for pearls in Hong Kong is that the best ones come from Japan. If you are looking for a serious set of pearls, find a dealer who will show you the Japanese government inspection certification that accompanies every legally exported pearl. Many pearls cross the border without one, and for a reason.

Pearls are usually sold loosely strung and are weighed by the *momme*. Each momme is equal to 3.75 grams. The size of the pearl is measured in millimeters. Size 3s are small, like caviar, and 10s are large, like mothballs. The average buyer is looking for something between 6 and 7 millimeters. The price usually doubles every half-millimeter after 6. Therefore, if a 6-millimeter pearl is $10, a 6.5-millimeter pearl would be $20, a 7-millimeter pearl $40, and so on. When the pearl gets very large, prices often triple and quadruple with each half millimeter.

Most pearls you will encounter are cultured. The pearl grower introduces a small piece of mussel shell into the oyster and then hopes that Mother Nature will do her stuff. The annoyed oyster coats the "intruder" with nacre, the lustrous substance that creates the pearl. The layers of nacre determine the luster and size. It takes about 5 years for an oyster to create a pearl. The oysters are protected from predators in wire baskets in carefully controlled oyster beds.

There are five basic varieties of pearls: freshwater, South Sea, *akoya,* black, and *mabe* (pronounced *maw*-bay). Freshwater pearls, also known as Biwa pearls, are Rice Krispies–shaped and come in shades of pink, lavender, cream, tangerine, blue, and blue-green. Many of the pearls larger than 10 millimeters are known as South Sea pearls. They are produced in the South Seas, where the water is warmer and the oysters larger. The silver-lipped oyster produces large, magnificent silver pearls. The golden-lipped oyster produces large golden-colored pearls.

The pearls you are probably most familiar with are known as *akoya* pearls. They range from 2 to 10 millimeters in size. The shapes are more round than not, and the colors range from shades of cream to pink. A few of these pearls have a bluish tone.

The rarest pearl is the black pearl, which is actually a deep blue or blue-green. Black-lipped oysters in the waters surrounding Tahiti and Okinawa produce these gems, which range in size from 8 to 15 millimeters. Putting together a perfectly matched set is difficult and costly.

Mabe pearls have flat backs and are considered "blister" pearls because of the way they are attached to the shell. They are distinguished by their silvery-bluish tone and rainbow luster.

Pearls are judged by their luster, nacre, color, shape, and surface quality. The more perfect the pearl in all respects, the more valuable. Test pearls by rolling them—cultured pearls are more likely to be perfectly round and will, therefore, roll more smoothly.

You needn't be interested in serious pearls, whether natural or fake. In fact, prices being what they are, I'm in favor of fakes. Fake versions of cultured pearls are readily available in Hong Kong; specialty items such as baroque-style or gray pearls are hard to come by. Chanel-style pearl items may be found in fashion stores, but not at pearl dealers.

Silk

Anthropologists will tell you that silk is China's single greatest contribution to world culture. The quality of Chinese silk has always been so superior that no substitute has ever been deemed acceptable. The trade routes that brought silk around the world also brought cultural secrets from ancient worlds into Europe.

The art of weaving silk originated some 4,000 years ago in China and has spread throughout Asia and the world. China, however, remains the largest exporter of silk cloth and garments. Hong Kong receives most of its silk fabric directly from China. Fabric shops in the markets sell rolls of silk for reasonable prices, although silk is not dirt cheap and may be priced competitively in your home market.

When buying silk, be sure that it is real. Many wonderful copies are on the market. Real silk thread burns like human hair and leaves a fine ash. Synthetic silk curls or melts as it burns. If you are not sure, remove a thread and light a match. If the dealer has a fit, ask him to do it or walk out. Vendors who are proud of their merchandise will often do the test for you. Ask.

Snuff Bottles

A favorite collector's item, snuff bottles come in porcelain, glass, stone, metal, bamboo, bronze, and jade. They also come in old and new old-style versions. They are hard to distinguish from perfume bottles, especially if they have no tops. In short, watch out; because of tourist demand, fakes flood this category.

A top-of-the-line collectible snuff bottle can go for $100,000; if you think you are buying a fine example of the art form for $10, think again. Glass bottles with carved overlays are rare and magnificent; there are specific schools of design and style in snuff bottles that are especially valuable to collectors. You can find more ordinary examples in any market. If you just want a few ornaments for the house (or Christmas tree), the markets or shops on Hollywood Road in Hong Kong will have plenty.

Soy Sauce

Ongoing disputes about soy sauce manufacturing have become a big brouhaha for grocery shoppers in the U.S., where Japan is demanding specific labels and a possible name change. The real thing must be made from real soy products and fermented for at least 3 months.

Spirit Money

Colorful fake paper money to be burned for the dead, spirit money is sold in old-fashioned paper shops, which are fast fading out. There are a string of paper shops on Shanghai Street in Kowloon; you can also find them in Causeway Bay near Jardine's Bazaar and in Macau, in the antiques-stores neighborhood.

Tea

The **Museum of Tea Ware in Flagstaff House,** Cotton Tree Drive, Hong Kong, is a good place to start exploring the mysteries of tea. Tea has been cultivated in China for more than 2,000 years and reflects the climate and soil where it is grown, much as European wines do. There are three categories of tea: unfermented, fermented, and semi-fermented.

It is customary to drink Chinese tea black, with no milk, sugar, or lemon. Cups do not have a handle, but often do have a fitted lid to keep the contents hot and to strain the leaves as you sip. Because Hong Kong was a British colony, many hotel lobbies and restaurants serve English high tea (a great opportunity to rest your feet and gear up for a few more hours of shopping).

Because tea is relatively inexpensive and often comes in an attractive package or tin, it makes an excellent gift, whether you choose high-priced, well-packaged goods or those from a grocery store or herbal or medicine shop. All the Chinese department stores have a wide selection of teas and tea containers.

Chapter Four

....

HONG KONG

WELCOME TO HONG KONG

....

Hong Kong is the center of the universe, the diamond in the Asian crown. It was the first of the Asian markets to come back from the slump; last fall's auctions at Christie's and Sotheby's Hong Kong branches set record prices for specialty sales in Asian art. Real estate is back up; the stores are cookin'. McDonald's is expanding, and Disneyland Asia should be open as you read this. More and more flights are winging into town; disease and disaster have been forgotten as Hong Kong wows visitors with its future and the fact that English is readily spoken and understood.

GET THERE NOW

....

The folks in Beijing have decreed that Shanghai is the new Hong Kong. Some Chinese publications consider Shenzen the new Hong Kong. Frankly, there's nothing wrong with the old Hong Kong . . . and a lot that's right.

The pressure is on to get to Hong Kong before it changes too dramatically. You want to be able to grasp what Hong Kong has been historically and to understand what all the fuss was about. See, we're talking sociology, not shopping.

Use Hong Kong as your base for exploring the new China. Remember these rules:

- Designer goods are 20% less expensive in Hong Kong than in mainland China.
- Hong Kong has been doing luxury and customer service for so long that they are second nature.
- For 99 years, English was the official language.
- If you are looking for Chinese atmosphere, you may find it more readily in parts of Hong Kong than in China's big cities, where the past is being torn down at an alarming rate. Hong Kong is a lot more than the Star Ferry and the skyline you've seen on billboards—there are scads of nearby islands and destinations that take the mooncake when it comes to charm.

The Lay of the Land

Hong Kong encompasses Hong Kong Island, the city of Kowloon, the New Territories, and a few hundred islands. Technically speaking, what we commonly refer to as Hong Kong is now part of the People's Republic of China (PRC), but because it has separate but equal status, its address is written as "Separate Administrative Region," or "SAR" (not to be confused with SARS, the disease).

When people discuss addresses in the Hong Kong area, they may cite a particular number on a particular street, but more often than not, you'll hear your fellow travelers simplifying directions by just naming a building and a neighborhood. And they play fast and loose with what constitutes a neighborhood. Some people call all of Victoria Island "Central" and all of the Kowloon Peninsula "Kowloon." While these terms are geographically incorrect, everyone seems to understand the system, so don't knock yourself out trying to be absolutely precise.

Shopping in Hong Kong concentrates heavily on two areas: Central, the main business "downtown" area on the Hong Kong

Island side, and Tsim Sha Tsui in Kowloon. Central is very upscale, civilized, businesslike, and modern. Tsim Sha Tsui (often written TST) is grittier and more active in a frenetic way.

See "Shopping Neighborhoods," (p. 72) for a detailed discussion of Hong Kong's shopping and commercial districts. When you become an old China hand, you'll decide which side of the harbor is more "you" or is more convenient to your business or shopping style. Smart visitors stay on both sides of the island and shop all corners.

BOOKING HONG KONG

The Hong Kong Tourist Association (HKTA) provides a great deal of useful information for travelers at no cost. It publishes pamphlets on almost every subject imaginable, many of which you can pick up as you exit passport control at Hong Kong International Airport.

The monthly *Official Hong Kong Guide* contains general information about the city, including listings of festivals, events, and exhibits. The HKTA also publishes a weekly newspaper called *Hong Kong This Week*. It contains news of events and shows, along with the usual ads for shops. It's free at major hotels and in HKTA offices.

Inside the free packet you can pick up at the airport is the A-O-A Map Directory. Maps show both building and street locations. Because so many addresses include the building name, street, and area, it makes finding an address simple.

GETTING THERE

When it comes to booking your plane tickets, there are a confusing number of possibilities, deals, routes, and reasons to go with any number of different plans (and planes).

Hong Kong Orientation

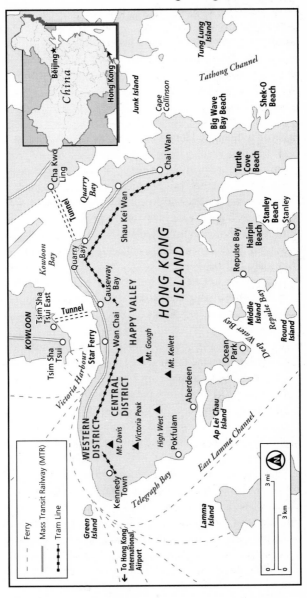

Ticket Deals

Because they buy in bulk, wholesalers often get better prices, and they pass their savings on to their customers. See p. 22 for a recommended agency in the U.S. and one in Paris. Both offer discounted deals.

Other thoughts:

- If you're flying to Hong Kong from the West Coast, look into a Circle Pacific fare or an All Asia ticket. Most American carriers, and many international ones, allow you to make your own itinerary, traveling to several cities in Asia at package-tour prices. You do not join a group; you set your own pace, but you get a break on the price because you fly all legs with the same carrier. I just saw a Cathay Pacific deal for $999 (when bought online) that offered a choice of some 17 cities.
- Treat yourself to a more comfortable seat than in coach. Most airlines offer an upgraded coach class, with extra legroom and amenities, called executive coach or some such fancy name.
- If you're pricing airfares on several carriers, it is imperative that you understand the quality of the service and what you are getting. Don't assume anything. Virgin has made quite a splash with its extra perks and great entertainment system, but it offers real value only to those travelers willing to pay extra for Upper Class service. (Double beds?!) Last time I flew Virgin, the seats that were not in Upper Class did not compete with other airlines' options for comfort or price.
- Consider the new technology. Flights now make it handily from the East Coast of the U.S. to Hong Kong—both Cathay Pacific and Continental do so.
- If you must fly in a coach seat, look for ways to break up the travel. You can get a discounted seat from the U.S. to London or Paris for $250, and a seat to Hong Kong for $600 to $700, leaving you enough money for a few nights in a hotel, a refreshing layover, and a bigger adventure.

- Package tours often offer the best deals financially, especially if they include airport transfers and some extras. Check them out, especially when you can stay at luxury hotels. Likewise, add-on tours offered by cruise lines sometimes have fabulous prices that include promotional events and benefits.
- If you are planning big-time shopping, base your ticket and class of service on excess baggage rules and costs.

PROMOTIONAL DEALS

All airlines have promotional deals. Deals to Asia are sometimes harder to find and often aren't advertised in America, but you can find them by calling the airlines' toll-free numbers in the United States or by going online. You may also find a promotional deal through your favorite bank card. And keep in touch with locals who can tip you off to promotional deals. Friends in Hong Kong recently told me about flights between Hong Kong and London that cost £200, round trip. They were available only for 3 days; all local carriers (Virgin, Cathay Pacific, and British Airways) matched the deal. The savings were for coach seats, but hey, what a deal.

An especially interesting new promotion called Fly Via HK (www.flyviahk.com) offers some amazingly low fares if you plan to make Hong Kong your hub. It includes various Chinese and Pacific Rim destinations and big-name carriers such as Cathay Pacific, Thai Airways, Philippine Airlines, and Dragonair. Fares are most often posted in U.S. dollars and include deals to nearby Cambodia and even Australia (for just $363—reason enough to put another shrimp on the barbie, mate).

Don't forget Disney deals, which offer packages to the newest Magic Kingdom and the happiest place in Asia. Disneyland Asia is near the airport on Lantau; you can take the train into the major shopping districts of Hong Kong and Kowloon. (The new Disney hotels won't be open until 2006 or 2007.) Also note there's plenty of shopping in the kingdom; Disney has closed its freestanding stores in Asia in order to encourage people to shop in the kingdom. There are some Disney souvenirs at the Hong Kong airport. For information about the park, visit www.hongkongdisneyland.com/eng.

AROUND-THE-WORLD DEALS

The deal of the century is very often an around-the-world ticket. One of the catches is that different-price tickets have different perks: The cheapest basic ticket allows you a set number of stops with any partner airlines affiliated with your carrier; you must always travel in one direction, but you can make side trips.

ARRIVING IN HONG KONG

The gorgeous Hong Kong airport, sometimes written HKIA, is modern and easy to use. Designed by Sir Norman Foster, it's a metallic crab sunning itself on Lantau Island. You flow without a care in the world along electric carpets, onto trains, and right through to the main terminal. Several modes of transportation run into town; follow signs in the grand entry hall.

If you have arranged car service from your hotel, look for the hotel desks in the center of the Arrivals Hall. Find the appropriate desk and check in; someone will escort you through the rest of the process, taking your baggage and meeting you at your car.

Car Service

Traveling from the airport in the swank car your hotel sends for you is a delightfully elegant way to arrive—and an expensive one. Although public transport is simple and inexpensive, part of the fun of being in Hong Kong is settling into the hotel's Rolls, Daimler, or Mercedes-Benz. Expect to pay $75 to $135 (it varies from hotel to hotel) each way for the luxury, but do try to find it in your budget. Hotels in the Central district—the main shopping and business area—may charge more than those in Kowloon.

Airport Bus & Train

AirBuses run every 15 minutes or so; another bus option is Executive Coach. The seating is nicer than the first-class cabin of any airline, with tons of legroom for you, your wheelchair, and your carry-on. You can reserve your place through your hotel or go to the bus desk in the A part of the arrivals hall. The fare to Central is HK$140 ($18).

The train (Airport Express) is for those who have little to no luggage; therefore, I've never used it. It whooshes right through the airport terminal, and you can hop on and be at the main station in Central in 22 minutes. From there, you can take a taxi to your hotel. You can buy a tourist package for HK$220 ($29) that includes the one-way Airport Express fare and a 3-day MTR Octopus Card. For HK$300 ($39), it includes the round-trip fare to the airport. You can even buy the pass from the duty-free on some airlines. If you don't buy the package, the bus costs HK$154 ($20) each way.

Taxis

Taxi stands are near the arrival lounge. A large sign lists approximate fares to different areas of Hong Kong and Kowloon. If you're confused, look for the transportation desk. Taxis usually charge a flat rate of approximately $45—it is a long drive to town. I took a taxi once and never did it again. Yeah, I was unlucky. The car stank of smoke, the driver was incredibly rude (he wanted to drop me across the street from my hotel, luggage and all), and—the last straw—he picked his nose with the same hand to reach for my change. I saved half the price of a hotel car, but the bus is so much more fun that I prefer to save more and float in executive luxury.

GETTING AROUND

Hong Kong is an easy city to navigate because its transportation options are excellent. It's a good city for walking, true, but you'll also want to enjoy its ferries, *kaidos* (bigger ferries), trams, double-decker buses, and superb MTR (Mass Transit Railway).

Most rides on the MTR take less than 20 minutes; you can cross the harbor in approximately 5 minutes. Do invest in an Octopus Card. The electronic signal is so strong that it can be read from your wallet or handbag, so you can flash and pass with ease.

Crossing the harbor by car or taxi during rush hour is hardest, but it's a breeze on the MTR or the Star Ferry, which takes almost the same amount of time. Don't ask me about the hour I spent in a taxi trapped inside the tunnel when I was too lazy to take public transportation.

MTR

The MTR stop at Central will get you to most locations in Hong Kong, and the Tsim Sha Tsui (TST) stop is convenient to most locations in Kowloon. *For a detailed map of Hong Kong Regional Transportation, see the inside back cover of this book.*

The MTR is half the fun of getting to great shopping. Three lines connect the New Territories to industrial Kwun Tong, to business Central, to shopping Tsim Sha Tsui, and to the residential eastern part of the island. Each station is color-coded, and signs are in English and Chinese.

The longest trip takes less than an hour, and the cost is based on the distance you travel. Buy your ticket at the station vending machines by looking for your destination and punching in the price code. You will need exact change, which you can get from a machine nearby. Ticket windows sell multiple-journey tickets.

If you're visiting Hong Kong from overseas, the best value is a tourist 1-day MTR ticket, available at any HKTA office, any MTR station, select Hang Seng banks, and MTR Travel Services Centres. It costs HK$50 ($6.50). You must buy your ticket within 2 weeks of your arrival and show your passport at the time you purchase it.

The 1-day option is for tourists; stored-value cards are called Octopus Cards. They cost HK$70 ($9.10), HK$100 ($13), and HK$200 ($26).

One-stop journeys usually cost HK$4 (50¢) to HK$10 ($1.30), depending on the distance; ticket boxes require exact change.

Octopus Cards are electronic and can be read through your wallet or handbag; just place yours on the pad. Flash it again to depart the station at your destination.

To use single-journey tickets, insert and retrieve. You need the ticket to exit the station. If you have a single-journey ticket, it will be "eaten."

The MTR runs between 6am and 1am. If you need to get somewhere earlier or later, take a taxi.

Taxis

Taxis in Hong Kong are cheap. The meter starts at HK$15 ($1.95); after that, the charge is HK$1.30 (20¢) per 200m (656 ft.). Taking the Cross-Harbour Tunnel costs an extra HK$10 ($1.30) each way, making the total additional fees HK$20 ($2.60). I tend to avoid taking a taxi through the Cross-Harbour Tunnel unless I'm loaded down with packages and have had a long, hard day of shopping. There are surcharges for luggage, waiting time, and radio calls.

If a taxi is in Central and has a sign saying KOWLOON, it means that the driver would like a fare going back to Kowloon and will not charge the extra HK$10 ($1.30) tunnel fee if he gets such a fare. It is sometimes hard to find a cab during the 4pm shift change. If a taxi doesn't stop for you on a busy road, it is probably because the driver is not allowed to stop.

Look for a taxi stand where you can pick up a cab. Hotels are always good places to find a taxi. Even if you are not staying at that hotel, the doorman will help you. Tip him HK$5 (65¢).

English is still an official language, but it's always nice insurance to have your destination written in Chinese. Hotels have preprinted cards; one side tells the driver how to reach the hotel. I was quite shocked on several different taxi trips when the drivers simply put a map book in my hand and asked me to find the address. If I didn't know my way around town, I would have been sunk. Save yourself the aggravation—get a card ahead of time.

Trains

The Kowloon-Canton Railway (KCR) serves the areas between Kowloon and the Chinese border. Because you can't get into China without a visa, chances are you won't be traveling as far as the border. But do hop onboard, because you should take this chance to get out into the New Territories and see some of the real world. If you have a visa (or want one) to visit Shenzen, step this way.

The new TST East station allows you to step out of the Peninsula or InterContinental hotel and into a luxury train that whisks you to China in less than an hour. For tips on visits across the border, see p. 18.

Ferries

The most famous of the Hong Kong ferries is the Star Ferry, with service from Kowloon to Central and back. The 8-minute ride is one of the most scenic in the world. You can see the splendor of Hong Kong Island's architecture and the sprawl of Kowloon's shore. The green-and-white ferries have connected the island to the peninsula since 1898.

Billed as the least expensive tourist attraction in the world, the Star Ferry is a small piece of magic for no more than pocket change. First class costs HK$2.20 (30¢); tourist class is HK$1.75 (25¢). The difference is minimal except at rush hour, when the upper deck (first class) is less crowded. The difference is maximized if you want to take pictures, because you get a much better view from the upper deck. The Central/Tsim Sha Tsui (TST) service runs daily from 6:30am to 11:30pm.

Note: The different classes have different entries; on the Kowloon side, they even have different shopping opportunities!

Trams

Watch out crossing the streets of Central, or you're likely to be run over by a double-decker tram. Island trams have operated for more than 85 years, from far western Kennedy Town to Shau Kei Wan in the east. They travel in a straight line, except for a detour around Happy Valley. The fare is HK$1 (10¢) for adults; half-price for children. You pay as you enter. Many trams do not go the full distance east to west, so note destination signs before getting on. Antique trams are available for tours and charters, as are the regular ones.

The Peak Tram has been in operation for more than 100 years. It is a must for any visitor to Hong Kong—unless you are afraid of heights. You can catch the tram behind the Hilton Hotel, on Garden Road. A free shuttle bus will take you from the Star Ferry or Central MTR station (Chater Garden exit) to the Peak Tram terminal. The tram runs to the Peak every 10 minutes starting at 7am and ending at midnight. The trip takes 8 minutes. At the top you hike around to various viewing points or peek in on some of the expensive mansions and high-rises. The best time to make this trip is just before dusk; you can see the island scenery on the trip up, walk around, watch the spectacular sunset, and then ride down as all the city lights are twinkling.

Rickshaws

It's over, folks. Rickshaws are *fini, kaput,* anachronistic, socially incorrect, gone with the wind.

Every now and then you can find someone near the Star Ferry terminal on the Hong Kong side to pose for a picture. The price for doing so is negotiable. The going rate is HK$70 ($9.10), but sometimes you can put HK$50 ($6.50) in the driver's hand for a few quick snaps.

SLEEPING IN HONG KONG

I can't think of any other city in the world—and that includes Paris—where your choice of hotel is a more integral part of your stay than in Hong Kong.

Although I'm incredibly picky about hotels, I've found several in Hong Kong that offer the most important factor in a shopping hotel—location—and still have all the luxury I lust after. Asian hotels are famous for their deluxe standards and fabulous service; enjoying these perks is part of the pleasure of staying in Hong Kong.

Hotel Tips

I find hotels' official rack rates irritating and refuse to quote them in these pages. Few people pay the official rates, and there are almost always deals to be made. Hong Kong is deal city.

Promotional rates can be as low as $149 a night at the Marco Polo Gateway (Kowloon); I once saw a Mandarin Oriental ad touting Oriental Interlude Leisure breaks, with a price per room (not per person) of HK$1,100 ($143). Rates are on the rise in Hong Kong, however, and rooms can be dear, especially when trade fairs are in town and hotels are full of convention-goers. It pays to shop around for rates and for the right time of year to visit because prices change with the seasons.

Tricks of the Trade

Some secrets that might make booking your hotel easier:

- Ask about packages, which may include breakfast, airport transfers, and other items that usually incur an extra charge. Almost every luxury hotel in the world offers a honeymoon package. As long as you don't show up with the kids, you're on your honeymoon.
- Mileage awards can be used to pay for hotel rooms, to obtain discounts on rooms, or to accrue more mileage for your favorite frequent-flier account.

- Always ask whether the hotel offers weekend or 5-day rates. Almost all hotels discount rooms during the off season or when there is not a lot of business in town. Hong Kong has so many conventions that you may get a low-price convention rate if you ask and rooms are available.
- Peak season in Hong Kong is October and November; you'll pay top dollar. Summer rates are usually the least expensive, and there are often discounts beginning the first week in December.
- Watch out for Japanese and Chinese holidays, which are usually not on U.S. and U.K. calendars; Hong Kong hotels fill at these times.
- Check the big chains for promotional rates. Often you can prepay in U.S. dollars and save, or the chain will have a deal in the computer that your travel agent doesn't know about. A Hilton telephone operator told me about an exceptional value at the Conrad. InterContinental has totally reinvented itself; find out what it offers. I do a Shop & Spa tour for InterContinental every year, which is a package deal with great prices. Join us!

Hong Kong's Best Shopping Hotels

CENTRAL

I've found three hotels that serve as one because they're in the same location: **Pacific Place,** right above the mall of the same name. They all have entrances within the mall as well as front doors on the street.

FOUR SEASONS HOTEL HONG KONG
8 Finance St., Central (MTR: Central)

Four Seasons returned to Hong Kong with this wow-'em hotel in September 2005. It's in the IFC Tower, overlooking the water and Kowloon. Look for promotional rates to celebrate the opening. The IFC Tower also houses a multilevel luxury shopping mall and cinema complex, and the Airport Express train station. U.S. and Canada reservations © **800/819-5053.**

Local © 852/3196-8888; fax 852/3196-8050. www.four
seasons.com/hongkong.

ISLAND SHANGRI-LA
Pacific Place, Supreme Court Rd., Central (MTR: Admiralty)

The first time I visited the Island Shangri-La was for Richard
Branson, who put me into the shopping-tour business. I fell
in love with this location, with the Pacific Place mall, and with
the exotic architecture and style of the Island Shangri-La.
Before understanding the hotel, I had thought that perhaps this
location wasn't convenient—wrong! Getting around by hopping in a taxi or even walking is easy, and I loved being
attached to one of the best malls in the city.

Note the **Marriott** and the **Conrad** hotels connect to the mall.
You may want to price all three hotels.

Room rates vary from about $150 to over $300 for the same
room, depending on the time of year and occupancy conditions. U.S. reservations © **800/942-5050.** Local © 852/2877-
3838; fax 852/2521-8742. www.shangri-la.com.

MANDARIN ORIENTAL
5 Connaught Rd., Central (MTR: Central)

I always considered myself a Kowloon person, but on my last
trip to Hong Kong I forced myself to stay at the Mandarin Oriental and was blown away by the services, conveniences, and
efficiency. It is truly the center of the universe. Even if you aren't
staying here, check it out: Go upstairs for cocktails and a
view, visit the coffee shop for lunch, have formal tea (it's a meal
unto itself), and shop in the hotel's mall. There's a branch of
Vong upstairs.

Mandarin Oriental has a forbiddingly formal reputation that
may lead you to believe you cannot afford it, but I beg you to
reconsider. During promotional periods, the hotel is practically
giving away rooms. I actually saw a listed promotional rate
of $150 per night, but $450 is more like the regular rate.

There's been a weekend promotion that offered a harbor-view room for Friday and Saturday nights only for $312; additional nights are $135. U.S. reservations © **800/526-6566.** Local © 852/2522-0111; fax 852/2810-6190. www.mandarin oriental.com.

Note: Sometime during the life of this book, the Mandarin Oriental will close for a total makeover. The boutique **Mandarin Landmark Hotel** will open inside the Landmark mall, across the street from the Mandarin Oriental, to take care of the hotel's regular guests during the refurbishment.

KOWLOON

Excelsior Hotel
281 Gloucester Rd., Causeway Bay (MTR: Causeway Bay)

I associate this very large hotel with visitors who don't care so much about glamour; they love the funky atmosphere of Causeway Bay, which attracts crowds of trendy young shoppers. Tour groups and first-timers tend to hide this hotel's sophistication.

A member of the Mandarin Oriental hotel family, the Excelsior costs less and charges less for its services—the car and driver to and from the airport, the business center, and so forth. And the breakfast buffet is downright amazing. There's an MTR station a block away, and there's more shopping than anyone can stand—local and luxe. Half a block away is my latest favorite spa: Big Bucket Foot, where you get a foot massage (in a big bucket) for $20. U.S. reservations © **800/526-6566.** Local © 852/2894-8888; fax 852/2576-7715. www.mandarin oriental.com.

Grand Stanford InterContinental
78 Mody Rd., TST East (MTR: TST East)

TST East is a location popular with business travelers who want to get into China easily. It's essentially right on top of the KRC Hung Hom train station, and an escalator ride from the new TST East train station.

InterContinental has this hotel in its constellation for those who don't need the luxury of the flagship property (see below) and are happy to get a room with the usual InterConti perks for about $150 to $185.

There's just enough shopping in the area to satisfy your needs, and you can walk to TST or take the ferry directly to Central. U.S. and Canada reservations © 888/303-1758. Local © 852/2721-5161; fax 852/2732-2233. www.interconti.com.

INTERCONTINENTAL HOTEL
18 Salisbury Rd., Kowloon (MTR: TST)

To me, it will always be the Regent, but locals have adapted to the change and call this hotel the InterConti. In one of the most scenic locations in Hong Kong, the hotel occupies the tip of Kowloon Peninsula; the views from the lobby bar at night are nothing short of spectacular.

The tricks and treats are also incredible—an Alain Ducasse restaurant; a club membership that provides for tons of perks, making it a bargain shopper's best buy; a Feng Shui spa; and the wonderful Yu, my favorite local seafood restaurant. Downstairs is one of my favorite quick-bite places—the coffee shop, Harbourside.

Rates here vary enormously; I have heard of $199 rooms during very low season. However, the average is closer to $300 and up (harbor views cost more, of course). U.S. and Canada reservations © 888/303-1758 or 770/604-2000. Local © 852/2721-1211; fax 852/2739-4546. www.interconti.com.

KOWLOON HOTEL
19–21 Nathan Rd., Kowloon (MTR: TST)

This hotel's secret? It's owned and operated by the Peninsula Group. It's next door to the Pen, in the middle of a shopping neighborhood, and it's in a slim tower, so some rooms have excellent views. The rates are half of those at the Pen, and sometimes less; I've seen $99 summer rates!

Because many guests are businesspeople, there are fax and computer terminals in the rooms and all sorts of electronic gadgets. You can print out your local newspaper, run to the Starbucks downstairs, enjoy the restaurants and promotional treats, and take advantage of the in-house Jurlique spa.

The bad news: Rooms are very, very small. U.S. reservations © **800/262-9467.** Local © 852/2929-2888; fax 852/2739-9811. www.peninsula.com.

LANGHAM HOTEL
8 Peking Rd., Tsim Sha Tsui (MTR: TST)

If you know the London hotel scene, you are familiar with the Langham Hotel, a former Hilton a block from Regent Street. This hotel—and its sister (Langham Place) in Mong Kok—shares the same ownership. You can spot the similarity as soon as you enter the Kowloon hotel; the lobby has a barrel-vaulted ceiling so Victorian in style that you can scarcely remember you are in Hong Kong.

The Langham is relatively new to the five-star scene, after a $30 million renovation that made it a luxury property aimed at business travelers. The confusing part is that the hotel is in the Leading Hotels of the World bible (from which I book most of my hotels), so you end up comparing it to the Peninsula, across the street. In reality, this hotel competes with the Inter-Conti and the recently spruced-up Sheraton.

The hotel is gorgeous; the 488 modern, plush rooms have every amenity. The Club floor offers even more perks, such as one-way airport transfer (included in the room rate).

Opposite the Ocean Terminal mall and the Hong Kong China City ferry terminal, the hotel is 1 block from the Star Ferry. It has several restaurants, including a New York–style deli. For the dish on the Chinese restaurant, T'ang Court, see p. 67. U.S. reservations © **800/457-4000,** or book through Leading Hotels of the World (© 800/223-6800). Local © 852/2375-1133. www.langhamhotels.com.

THE PENINSULA HOTEL
Salisbury Rd., Kowloon (MTR: TST)

The Pen, as it is called, is the most famous hotel in Hong Kong. In the ever-changing world of hotel competition, this *grande dame* keeps ahead with new and imaginative programs. The latest development, the Peninsula Academy, allows you to take exclusive classes, hear lectures, meet with specialists, or eat in the chef's private kitchen. The newer part of the hotel, a tower with superb views, a health club, a pool, and a Philippe Starck–designed restaurant (Felix), provides modern fancy to go with old-world 1928 fancy. And yes, there's a helicopter pad on the roof, and you can have a Rolls-Royce transfer to or from the airport.

Not only is there a complete shopping mall in the hotel, but there's also a wonderful health club and Clarins spa—my jet-lag well-being treatment there actually saved my life. I now book myself into the spa shortly after arrival. In fact, the perfect way to get acclimated is to shop in the hotel arcade and then slip into Clarins. Finish up with tea in the famed lobby.

With these extras, you already know this is the most expensive hotel in town. A bargain rate would be in the low $300s, but sometimes you'll find promotions that offer a free night or some other nicety. U.S. reservations © **800/262-9467**, or book through Leading Hotels of the World (© 800/223-6800). Local © 852/2920-2888; fax 852/2722-4170. www.peninsula.com.

SECRETS OF THE FOUR STARS

Anyone looking for a great hotel with a convenient shopping location and a price break would do well to learn this secret: Many of the biggest names in town have secondary hotels. These hotels do not serve the same market and are usually business hotels, but they have great management programs and excellent rates.

DINING IN HONG KONG

If you think Hong Kong is most famous for shopping, think again. The number one attraction is culinary pleasures—from five-star restaurants in the most elegant hotels to Chinese eateries somewhat off the beaten path. Certain places are so fabulous that you just have to try them to complete your Hong Kong experience. True foodies may even want to book a trip to coincide with the Hong Kong Food Festival in August.

Because this is a small town and food is so important to the culture, there are a number of private dining clubs. If you don't know a member, ask your hotel concierge if he can book you a table at either **Kee Club** or **China Club**.

Legends & Landmarks

When I pick a restaurant for this category, I consider a combination of factors: the length of time the establishment has been in operation, the quality of its food, location, and ambience. Some places so typify what is special about Hong Kong that I consider them "don't miss" experiences. A few (such as Jumbo) are good for the family, for first-timers, or for people who want an entire experience that includes food. In fact, all of the places in this section are legends, landmarks, or both, and are worthy of a memory-making meal.

GADDI'S
The Peninsula Hotel, Salisbury Rd., Kowloon (MTR: TST)

Visitors and locals alike know Gaddi's as the best French restaurant in town, and serious foodies wouldn't consider a trip to Hong Kong complete without a visit. It's much like a private club of local and visiting professionals.

If you are looking for something else (meal included), you may want to book lunch or dinner at the chef's private table in the kitchen. You can ask the chef to create a menu for you, or you can pick from the regular menu. If the kitchen table is booked, note that some people request the kitchen menu for lunch in the restaurant.

Lunch and dinner are both popular; lunch is less expensive. However, leave it to me to find a few deals: The house offers a set dinner menu of five courses, each with its own wine, for approximately $125 a person, an excellent value. Reservations are a must; call © 852/2366-6251.

JUMBO KINGDOM
Shum Wan, Aberdeen (no nearby MTR)

My first thought about Jumbo was that only tour groups go here, and it wasn't worth my time. It took me years to get up the nerve to come here, and now that I've done it, I feel like a fool. Why did I wait so long? If ever there was a fantasy place to bring your kids, this is it.

Jumbo, as you may already know, is the most famous of the floating restaurants in Aberdeen Harbour. It is best seen at night when all the lights are aglow, but you can go for lunch and take advantage of the souvenir vendors who set up shop in junks and on the pier that provides service from Aberdeen Harbour to the floating restaurant. (There's more shopping when you get into the restaurant, but all the prices are marked in yen.)

The place is enormous and has a fun, almost silly atmosphere. This is not intimate dining, but if dressing up in a mandarin's outfit and having your photo taken sounds like fun to you (or your kids), this is the place. Menus feature pictures, so you just point to what you want. The food is American-style Chinese. Dinner for two with beer is about $40. For reservations, call © 852/2553-9111.

LUK YU TEAHOUSE
24 Stanley St. (MTR: Central)

It's not the teahouse of the August Moon, but Luk Yu—a landmark eatery in the center of Central—could be a movie set. Order dim sum from the menu in Chinese, and try not to take pictures, because that's what everyone else is doing. Go for an early lunch (locals eat between 1 and 4pm, so if you're there by noon, you should be able to get a table without much of a wait) or at teatime, when you can get a table easily.

Dim sum is served until 5pm. A perfect location in Central makes this a good stop for shoppers; it's halfway to Hollywood Road and not that far from the Landmark.

Do note that waiters at Luk Yu make it a policy to be rude to Westerners unless they know you. On the other hand, it's rude for you to ask about the recent gangland shoot-'em-up. Dim sum meals will run about $20 per person; full meals cost more. For reservations, call © **852/2523-5464.** Cash only.

SPOON
InterContinental Hotel, 18 Salisbury Rd., Kowloon (MTR: TST)

Alain Ducasse's Spoon is a little fancier than its sibling in Paris, but certainly not as fancy as Ducasse's multistarred palace restaurants. The cooking is fusion, there's a mix-and-match menu, and the view is almost as good as the food. Prices are about $50 per person. For reservations, call © **852/ 2721-1211.**

T'ANG COURT
Langham Hotel, 8 Peking Rd., Kowloon (MTR: TST)

Classic Chinese food prepared as finely as any French cuisine. I had one of the most incredible meals of my life here: Not only was the food delish, but the meal was balanced in a way that glorified sweet and salty, crunchy and tender, texture and form. The crowd is somewhat dressy; reservations (© **852/2375-1133**) are advised.

Fast-Food Notes

If this kind of conservatism is not your cup of tea and you'd like to watch your purse (or you have the kids with you!), there are tons of franchised American fast-food joints in Hong Kong. You'll have no trouble finding a **McDonald's** or **KFC** anywhere you turn.

One night in Kowloon, we found a local diner where there were no other *gwailo* (foreigners) and then went for a stroll on Nathan Road and had dessert from **Häagen-Dazs**—and I didn't feel as though I'd sold out on the local experience in the slightest.

Snack & Shop

It's quite easy to get a snack while shopping in Hong Kong. It's simply a question of how adventurous you are. *Dai pai dong* is the Chinese name for the street vendors who cook food from carts in street markets or on corners. Although I have pictures of my sister, the late great Dr. Debbie, eating from assorted *dai pai dong,* her advice to me on how to stay healthy has remained in the back of my head: "Always eat lunch in the best hotel in town."

Hong Kong has lots of great hotels, and each has several restaurants, so you'll have no trouble following this simple advice.

Even the most expensive hotels usually have a coffee shop or a moderately priced restaurant amid their galaxy of four or five eateries. For a shopper's lunch, I'm often at:

HARBOURSIDE
InterContinental Hong Kong, 18 Salisbury Rd., Kowloon (MTR: TST)

My favorite chicken salad is off the menu, but I can cope because the view here is so fantastic that it is reason enough to stop by. One floor below the main lobby, the cafe is a fancy coffee shop for meals and snacks. Expect to spend about $15 per person, or you can do the buffet for about $50 per person. © 852/2721-1211.

THE LOBBY
The Peninsula Hotel, Salisbury Rd., Kowloon (MTR: TST)

The Pen is known for its other famous eateries (Felix, Gaddi's, and lunch at the chef's table in the kitchens), but the Lobby is a great place for a light bite and an opportunity to "do" the Pen, even on a budget. Tea is the big deal, and people do wait in line. I often come here for dinner. I get spaghetti or a salad for about $15. Easy, well priced, and near the Nathan Road shopping district. © 852/2920-2888.

MANDARIN ORIENTAL COFFEE SHOP
Mandarin Oriental Hotel, 5 Connaught Rd. (MTR: Central)

Shopper's heaven in terms of location, people-watching, and simple fare at not-too-high prices. The coffee shop is at the rear of the hotel, across from the Landmark and about half a block from the Armani shop. Also good for breakfast, tea, snacks, or just resting up when you're exhausted. You can do lunch for $15 a person. © 852/2522-0111.

SHOPPING HONG KONG

Shopping Hours

Generally, shops open late in the morning and stay open until late in the evening. Most specialty stores open at 10am and close at 6:30pm. However, these are just guidelines. Some stores open whenever they feel like it. Central businesses tend to open later than those in Kowloon.

For the most part, stores close at 6:30pm in Central, 7:30pm in Tsim Sha Tsui, and 9pm on Nathan Road in Yau Ma Tei and in Mong Kok. In all honesty, I've been in the stores on Granville Road until 11pm at night. I think that as long as there is traffic, the stores are willing to stay open.

Mall stores are open during regular business hours on Sunday. Most shops in the main shopping areas of Tsim Sha Tsui and Causeway Bay are open daily. Those in Central close on Sunday.

Many shops close on major public holidays. Everything closes on Chinese New Year; some stores are closed for 2 days, others for 2 weeks. Do not plan to be in Hong Kong and do any shopping at this time. The stores that remain open charge a premium. The stores where you want to shop will all be closed.

Store hours are affected by the following public holidays:

- January 1 (New Year's Day)
- January/February (Chinese New Year)
- March/April (Good Friday, Easter Sunday and Monday)
- June (Dragon Boat Festival)
- August 25 (Liberation Day)
- December 25 (Christmas) and December 26 (Boxing Day)

On public holidays, banks and offices close, and shops may close as well. Factory outlets will definitely not be open. Many holiday dates change from year to year. For specific dates, contact the HKTA before you plan your trip.

If you are planning a tour of the factory outlets, remember that lunch hour can fall anywhere between noon and 2pm, although 1 to 2pm is most common. Outlet shops will close for 1 hour, along with the factory. Because of this practice, you might as well plan to have lunch then, too.

Department store hours differ from store to store. The larger ones, like Lane Crawford and Chinese Arts & Crafts, maintain regular business hours: 10am to 5pm. The Japanese department stores in Causeway Bay open between 10 and 10:30am and close between 9 and 9:30pm. They're all closed on different days 1 day of the week, however, which can be confusing. Don't assume because one department store is closed that they all are.

Market hours are pretty standard. Only food markets (sometimes called "wet markets") open very early in the morning. There's no point in arriving in Stanley before 9am. Even 9:30am is slow; many vendors are still opening up. The Jade

Market opens at 10am every day, including Sunday, and closes around 3pm. The weekend street market on Reclamation Street is a local market, so it opens earlier; there's plenty going on at 9am.

Christmas in Hong Kong

Even when I'm in Hong Kong in July, I start thinking about Christmas. Christmas decorations go up in Kowloon (it's hard to spot the neon amid all the neon) in mid-November, when stores begin their Christmas promotions.

Christmas permeates the air; even street markets sell decorations—plastic wreaths, silk flowers, ornaments, and more. You'll also be thrilled to find Victorian-style embroidered tree ornaments in stores in Hong Kong.

Among the best deals in town at this time of year is the free shipping many department stores offer. It covers shipping to the United Kingdom or to anyplace in the world, depending on the store, for purchases that cost more than a certain amount.

Better yet, Hong Kong is the perfect place to load up on inexpensive presents. What can you find at home that's fabulous for less than $1? Not much! Go to the Jade Market and you'll find plenty.

New Year in Hong Kong

I don't mean Western New Year's; I mean Chinese New Year, and when it comes, you may go crazy if you want to shop. Expect most stores to be closed a minimum of 2 to 3 days, but some stores close for weeks. The date of the new year varies because it is based on a lunar calendar; the danger zone falls somewhere between the end of January and mid-February. In 2006, the big day is January 29; in 2007, it's February 18.

Hong Kong on Sale

The best thing about the sales in Hong Kong is that they are the best time to get regular retail merchandise—and designer brands—at the lowest prices. The real bargains in Hong Kong are not in retail stores; the real bargains in Hong Kong may not be in perfect condition. So if you insist on brand-new, clean, undamaged goods, you should feel safe buying them on sale. If you have teens or are on a limited clothing budget, shop Hong Kong during the sale periods. Check the advertisements in the *South China Morning Post* for special sale announcements.

Fakes for Sale

New York's streets teem with vendors selling faux Chanel earrings, T-shirts, and scarves. These goods are easy to differentiate from the real thing. While Hong Kong doesn't have a lot of fake Chanel on the streets (it's hidden), there are many items for sale—especially at markets—that appear to be real. But they aren't. They usually hold up in the same way you'd expect a fake to hold up—not well.

I once bought a canvas-and-leather book bag from a street market for the high (for Hong Kong) price of $20. It had a big, perfect Gap label on the front. It fell apart 36 hours later. Both buckles and one leather strap broke so quickly (in three different incidents) that I am convinced that real Gap labels were sewn onto rather ordinary canvas bags. Let the buyer beware.

The biggest change in the atmosphere comes from mainland China, where locals and tourists alike are flocking to Shenzen (and beyond) to snap up fakes for bargain prices. See p. 149 for details about Shenzen.

SHOPPING NEIGHBORHOODS

The island of Hong Kong (Central) and Kowloon (TST), on the Kowloon Peninsula, are the most popular areas and the two basic shopping neighborhoods.

Just because they are the best-known and the handiest areas doesn't mean you should stop learning your neighborhoods. I will send you everywhere, from TST East to the New

Territories; I'll also tell you how to reach some factory districts and a lot of other neighborhoods.

The more I visit Hong Kong, the more comfortable I am with getting away from tourists and the commercial main streets of Central and Kowloon. I define a successful visit to Hong Kong as one in which I've spent at least a little bit of time in the real-people neighborhoods. But I also have to admit that during my last trip to Hong Kong, with only 4 full days in town, anything in an out-of-the-way neighborhood quickly disappeared from my must-do list.

Getting Around the Neighborhoods

The MTR will get you almost everywhere, or at least into the main neighborhoods and basic shopping areas. Unless I specifically note otherwise in an address, the MTR stop at Central gets you to most locations in Hong Kong; use the MTR stop at Tsim Sha Tsui (TST) for most Kowloon shopping areas.

There is excellent bus and ferry service to outlying islands where you can roam around upon arrival. Getting to specific addresses in the New Territories can be difficult without a car; consider hiring a taxi or a car (with driver) from your hotel.

If your time is limited and you want to see a lot, a car and driver is an economical luxury. The price ranges from $250 to $350 per day. If you can't afford the whole day, hire the car and driver until lunch, and finish on foot. The time you'll save with a chauffeur will permit you to get to a number of out-of-the-way neighborhoods and enhance your enjoyment of the shopping time you have.

A Word About Addresses

An address is most often the name of the building and not the street address. I want to stress that when street addresses are written out, they may designate a specific door or portion of a building. So you may see different addresses for the same building, like the **Landmark, Swire House,** or **Prince's Building.** Don't assume it's an error. Simply check your trusty map. If an office building takes up a city block, as many do, shops can list different street addresses on all four sides!

The same is true when cruising the boutiques in a shopping center like the **Landmark:** Often the shop's address will simply be the name of the building. The easiest way to find what you're looking for is to check the directory on the main floor of the mall.

Hong Kong Island Neighborhoods

The island of Hong Kong makes up only a portion of what most tourists refer to as Hong Kong. While government, business, and "downtown" functions take place on the island, much of the local population lives elsewhere in neighborhoods that do not seriously feature shopping and, therefore, do not appear in these pages.

A ridge of hills topped by the famous Peak divides the island. The rich and famous live in villas lining the road to the Peak; the almost rich and famous (as well as the upper-middle class) live in what's called the "Mid-Levels," the area of the hills above Central but below the Peak.

To get to most other portions of the island, you can either go through a tunnel under the hills toward Aberdeen, or take the tram or MTR along the shoreline to the housing estates, where middle-class people live in housing blocks and "mansion" or "estate" developments.

CENTRAL

Central is the part of Hong Kong that refers to what we used to call "downtown" when I was growing up. It's the main business and shopping part of town, and the core of Hong Kong Island.

Shopping in Central is mostly Westernized and even glitzy. But wait, you round a corner and, voilà—it's the **Lanes:** real people galore. You walk up Pottinger to Hollywood Road, and, again—the real thing. Central seems to house the ridiculous and

Central & Western Districts

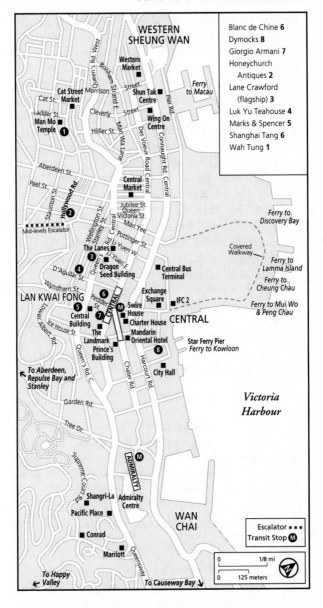

WESTERN
SHEUNG WAN

Western
Market

Ferry
to Macau

Shun Tak
Centre

Wing On
Centre

Cat Street
Market

Cat St.

Ladder St.

Man Mo
Temple ❶

Hillier St.

Aberdeen St.

Peel St.

Hollywood Rd.

Central
Market

Jubilee St.
Queen
Victoria St.

Man Yee

Mid-levels Escalator

The Lanes ❸

Dragon
Seed Building

Central Bus
Terminal

Ferry to
Discovery Bay

Covered
Walkway

Ferry to
Lamma Island

Ferry to
Cheung Chau

Ferry to Mui Wo
& Peng Chau

D'Aguilar St. ❹

Wyndham St.

LAN KWAI FONG

❻

Exchange
Square

IFC 2

Swire
House

Central
Building

❼

Charter House

CENTRAL

❺

The
Landmark

Prince's
Building

Mandarin
Oriental Hotel

❽

Star Ferry Pier
Ferry to Kowloon

To Aberdeen,
Repulse Bay and
Stanley

City Hall

Garden Rd.

Tree Dr.

Victoria
Harbour

ADMIRALTY

Shangri-La

Admiralty
Centre

Pacific Place

WAN
CHAI

Conrad

Marriott

To Happy
Valley

To Causeway Bay

Blanc de Chine **6**
Dymocks **8**
Giorgio Armani **7**
Honeychurch
  Antiques **2**
Lane Crawford
  (flagship) **3**
Luk Yu Teahouse **4**
Marks & Spencer **5**
Shanghai Tang **6**
Wah Tung **1**

Escalator ▪ ▪ ▪
Transit Stop Ⓜ

0   1/8 mi
0   125 meters

the sublime within the same city block; it's your opportunity to mix Westernized shopping with Eastern lifestyles.

The **Landmark** (see map), a shopping mall of mythic proportions, houses five floors of shopping, including stores in the basement, at street level, on a mezzanine, and in two towers that rise above the main floors. European designers have their shops here or across the street in **Swire House,** the **Prince's Building,** or the **Mandarin Oriental Hotel. Giorgio Armani,** across the street from the **Landmark,** is a knockout and brings a good bit of energy to this corner of Central.

The **Lanes** are two little alleys (Li Yuen West and Li Yuen East; see map) half a block apart and teeming with people and products. They are lined with storefronts and filled with stalls, so you have to look behind the stalls and poke into nooks and crannies to get the full flavor. One lane specializes in handbags (mostly imitations of famous brands and styles, few of good quality); the other, underwear.

The **Pedder Building** (p. 120) is conveniently located across the street from the Landmark and in every shopper's direct path. There are a handful of factory outlets and jobbers here, as well as the tony **Blanc de Chine. Shanghai Tang** is also here, alongside the outlet building: This is the single best stop if you need a visual pick-me-up and a piece of oh-wow retailing.

WESTERN

The Western District is adjacent to Central and can be reached on foot or by MTR. Take the MTR to Sheung Wan to get to central Western. Despite the decidedly touristy flavor in the renovation of **Western Market,** the Western District is a lot more Chinese, in both appearance and attitude, than Central. This is the district to see before it is ruined; as modernization continues, Western in its current form will disappear within the next few years.

Going west from Central, the area begins shortly after **Central Market,** at Possession Street, and continues to Kennedy Town, where most of the local working people live. Western includes the famous **Man Wa Lane,** where you can purchase your own personalized chop (p. 98), the **Shun Tak Centre** (where you take the ferry to Macau), and **Bonham Strand East,** where you'll find scores of Chinese herbalists. The farther west you wander, the more exotic the area becomes.

My best way of "doing" Western is to combine it with a trip to Hollywood Road; if you walk downhill from Hollywood Road, you'll end up in Western. Then you can take in the **Western Market** before walking back to Central or hopping on the MTR at Shun Tak station.

HOLLYWOOD ROAD

Up above Central, and technically within the Central District, Hollywood Road—Hong Kong's antiques district—is a shopping neighborhood unto itself. It isn't hard to get to, but it is not necessarily on the way to anywhere else you're going, so it's essential that you specifically plan your day or half a day to include this outing. You can reach it from the Central or Sheung Wan MTR stop. It's within walking distance if you're wearing sensible shoes and have the feet of a mountain goat; you can also tell your taxi driver *"By Fa Gai"* (meaning "white flower") and be dropped off in the core of the antiques area, in what used to be the neighborhood where the prostitutes plied their trade.

There are antiques stores elsewhere, but Hollywood Road is still a great place to get to know. The idea is to walk the 3 blocks of Hollywood Road from Wyndham to the Man Mo Temple. Then you'll hit Cat Street and the flea market before descending into Western.

As charming as this area is, I must warn you up front that much of what is in these shops is imitation, or at least faux. If you are looking to do anything more serious than browse, I suggest you make your first stop **Honeychurch Antiques** (no. 29). Expatriate American owners Glenn and Lucille Vessa are bright, honest, and always willing to help. They know who's who and what's what in their world of dealers and will tell you about their stock and everyone else's. Their look is an eclectic blend of antiques from around the Orient (kind of country chinoiserie); however, they know who has the more formal pieces. In fact, they know who has everything. If you are spending big bucks, it is imperative that you buy from a reputable shop. Ask Glenn and Lucille for guidance.

But wait! **Wah Tung,** the porcelain shop, has a showroom on Hollywood Road (no. 148), and although I think it is overpriced, there's a lot to be said for convenience. The entrance is small and not very warm; you may be put off. Go upstairs.

WAN CHAI

Wan Chai these days means "Convention Center," but it is also a showcase for the cutting-edge set. The area that was once known as the home of Susie Wong and then better known for the Hyatt hotel is now getting trendy. Start with **Fine Man,** 123 Wan Chai Rd., and work your way to **Conrad,** 288 Wan Chai Rd. Stores are also popping up on Hennessy Road, in the Wan Chai district but not on Wan Chai Road.

Note that if you are at a convention in the Convention Center, you have a lot of walking to do to get to any decent shopping. The **Chinese Arts & Crafts** store is nearest; everything else is a big schlep.

The Star Ferry provides direct access from Kowloon Peninsula: It travels from Tsim Sha Tsui to Wan Chai Pier. Old Wan Chai has been pushed back from the waterfront and will continue to be developed. If you want to see some original architecture and shops, prowl Queen's Road East and the lanes connecting it to Johnston Road. Shopping in the convention center is decidedly unexciting, but if you move on to the Hopewell Building, there is a fabulous **street market** on nearby Fenwick Street—no other tourists in sight, and a great place for taking pictures.

CAUSEWAY BAY

Oh me! Oh my! This area is so crowded, so fast-paced, so hip, and so much fun that I feel 20 years younger when I wander

Causeway Bay

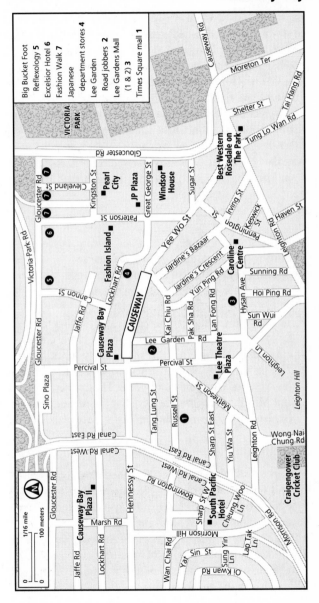

Big Bucket Foot Reflexology **5**
Excelsior Hotel **6**
Fashion Walk **7**
Japanese department stores **4**
Lee Garden Road jobbers **2**
Lee Gardens Mall (1 & 2) **3**
Times Square mall **1**

VICTORIA PARK

Moreton Ter

Causeway Rd

Shelter St

Tai Hang Rd

Tung Lo Wan Rd

Gloucester Rd

Best Western Rosedale on The Park

Kingston St

Pearl City

JP Plaza

Great George St

Windsor House

Sugar St

Irving St

Keswick Rd

Haven St

Leighton Rd

Cleveland St

Gloucester Rd

Paterson St

Yee Wo St

Pennington St

Fashion Island

Jardine's Bazaar

Jardine's Crescent

Caroline Centre

Sunning Rd

Victoria Park Rd

Lockhart Rd

Causeway Bay Plaza

CAUSEWAY

Kai Chiu Rd

Pak Sha Rd

Yun Ping Rd

Lan Fong Rd

Hysan Ave

Hoi Ping Rd

Sun Wui Rd

Cannon St

Jaffe Rd

Gloucester Rd

Lee Garden Rd

Lee Theatre Plaza

Leighton Ln

Leighton Hill

Sino Plaza

Percival St

Percival St

Matheson St

Sharp St East

Wong Nai Chung Rd

Tang Lung St

Russell St

Canal Rd East

Canal Rd West

Yiu Wa St

Leighton Rd

Craigengower Cricket Club

Hennessy St

Bowrington Rd

Canal Rd West

Sharp St W

Cheung Woo Ln

Morrison Rd

South Pacific Hotel

Morrison Hill

Causeway Bay Plaza Ii

Marsh Rd

Jaffe Rd

Lockhart Rd

Gloucester Rd

Wan Chai Rd

Yat Sin St

Sung Yin Ln

Oi Kwan Rd

Lap Tak Ln

Morrison Rd

N

1/16 mile

100 meters

the streets wondering why I've been such a stick-in-the-mud to stay in more established areas. Causeway Bay features one deluxe hotel (the **Excelsior**) and many tourist package–style hotels. It has several fancy Western malls, a street of outlet stores (Lee Gardens Rd.), some curving little alleys and streets filled with funk and glory, and countless shoppers, pushing their way to low-priced copies of the latest fashions. This area is far funkier than Central, but it does have **Chanel** and a branch of every other designer, if that's your thing. The MTR stop is Causeway Bay. Note that Causeway Bay is directly across the bay from Tsim Sha Tsui East, so getting through the Cross Harbour Tunnel is a tad easier.

Why do I love Causeway Bay?

- Funky street shopping, with a nod toward fashion, just-starting-out talent, and Japanese designers.
- Jardine's Bazaar, a small warren of street stalls.
- Fashion Walk, a gathering of designer and up-and-coming designer shops in three adjoining buildings.
- Times Square, a relatively new giant mall that has taken the town by storm because it has four floors of local and Western brands. My favorite store there is City Super.
- The Japanese department stores, which are less and less Japanese and more and more global. The two best are **Sogo** and **Mitsokoshi. Seibu,** the Bergdorf Goodman of Japanese department stores, is in the Pacific Place mall.

AP LEI CHAU

Some people think that this neighborhood is part of Aberdeen, but it is a place unto itself, connected to Aberdeen by a bridge. One high-rise building is home to many outlets, including the **Joyce Warehouse** (closed Mon) and the **Lane Crawford Warehouse.** For more furniture, try **Beijing Antiques Shop,** on the 20th floor, which has the kind of furniture many people cross into China to buy; it looks antique but is mostly refinished. Nearby is a Prada outlet, **Space.**

This is mostly a residential area, popular for its water views. Take a taxi and either have the driver wait or get the number of a taxi company so you can arrange a pick-up.

STANLEY/REPULSE BAY/OCEAN PARK

It seems to be very "in" to bash **Stanley Market** and say it isn't up to the old standards. I have a love-hate relationship with this tourist trap, which sits in the heart of downtown Stanley (no MTR; take a taxi or bus no. 6). Last trip, I loathed it. I actually had tears streaming down my face. It's very touristy, and I couldn't find anything to buy.

However, when I spoke to some British first-timers a week later, they couldn't stop raving about Stanley. And my Hong Kong shopping friends still claim to find bargains here. Maybe it's a matter of perspective.

Part of the pleasure of a visit to Stanley is the drive across the island, especially the view as you go around some of those coastal curves. If you agree with me about Stanley, simply get back in the taxi, go to Repulse Bay, shop the snazzy stores, eat lunch, and then return to Hong Kong proper.

Stanley is exceedingly crowded on the weekends, delightfully quiet midweek. Note that Stanley is not one of those markets where the early bird gets the worm. The early bird gets to sit and sulk until the shops open around 9:30am.

Kowloon Neighborhoods

Kowloon is packed with shops, hotels, excitement, and bargains. You can shop its more than 10 sq. km (4 sq. miles) for days and still feel that you haven't even made a dent. Like Hong Kong Island, Kowloon is the sum of many distinct neighborhoods.

TSIM SHA TSUI

The tip of Kowloon Peninsula consists of two neighborhoods: Tsim Sha Tsui and Tsim Sha Tsui East. It is home to most of Hong Kong's fine hotels and to Kowloon's serious tourist shopping. The MTR's Tsim Sha Tsui (TST) station is in the heart of things. Use the Jordan Road station when you're traveling a bit farther into Kowloon and working your way out of the tourist neighborhoods.

At the very tip of Tsim Sha Tsui are the Star Ferry Terminal and the Harbour City Complex. This western harborfront includes Ocean Terminal, Ocean Galleries, Ocean Centre, the Marco Polo Gateway Hotel, the Marco Polo Hong Kong Hotel, and the Marco Polo Prince Hotel.

The heart of Tsim Sha Tsui is **Nathan Road,** Kowloon's main shopping drag; it's the equivalent of London's Oxford Street. Nathan Road stretches from the waterfront for quite some distance and works its way into the "real people" part of Kowloon in no time at all. The most concentrated shopping is in the area called the **Golden Mile,** which begins on Nathan Road perpendicular to Salisbury Road. Both sides of this busy street are jam-packed with stores, arcades, covered alleys, and street vendors. There are also some hotels here, each with a shopping mall and enough neon to make Las Vegas blush.

If you are walking north (away from the harbor), you'll pass the Golden Mile. Then you reach a mosque on your left and then the **Park Lane Shopper's Boulevard,** also on your left. To your right, across the street from the Park Lane, is **Burlington Arcade.** The next street on your right is **Granville Road,** which is famous for its jobbers, where brand-name goodies are sold from bins, although the bargain ops on this street have been going downhill at a fast pace.

Nathan Road is the core of Kowloon, but my favorite part of Tsim Sha Tsui is a bit off the beaten path—though directly in sight. In the Golden Mile section of Tsim Sha Tsui, two streets run parallel to Nathan Road and are centered between the Golden Mile and Ocean Terminal: Hankow Road and Haiphong Road. They have some outlets, some jobbers, and several stores that sell DVDs. Also check out Lock Road, which runs perpendicular to these streets. Once you become an old China hand, you'll note that prices on Nathan Road are for tourists, and you may disdain the whole Golden Mile area.

The Kowloon Peninsula

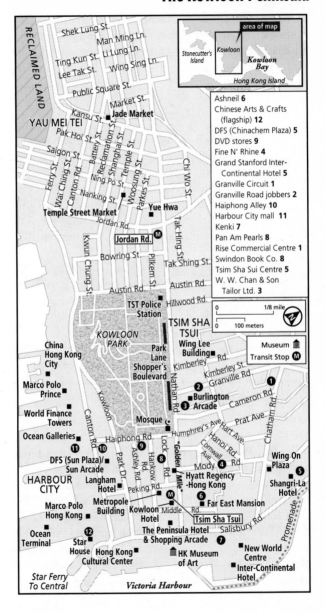

area of map

Stonecutter's Island

Kowloon

Kowloon Bay

Hong Kong Island

Ashneil **6**
Chinese Arts & Crafts (flagship) **12**
DFS (Chinachem Plaza) **5**
DVD stores **9**
Fine N' Rhine **4**
Grand Stanford Inter-Continental Hotel **5**
Granville Circuit **1**
Granville Road jobbers **2**
Haiphong Alley **10**
Harbour City mall **11**
Kenki **7**
Pan Am Pearls **8**
Rise Commercial Centre **1**
Swindon Book Co. **8**
Tsim Sha Sui Centre **5**
W. W. Chan & Son Tailor Ltd. **3**

RECLAIMED LAND

Shek Lung St.
Man Ming Ln.
Ting Kun St. Li Lung Ln.
Lee Tak St. Wing Sing Ln.
Public Square St.
Market St.
Kansu St.
YAU MEI TEI
Pak Hoi St.
Saigon St.
Wai Ching St.
Canton Rd.
Ferry St.
Battery St.
Reclamation St.
Shanghai St.
Temple St.
Woosung St.
Parkes St.
Ning Po St.
Nanking St.
Jade Market
Chi Wo St.
Yue Hwa
Temple Street Market
Yue Hwa
Jordan Rd.
Jordan Rd. Ⓜ
Tak Hing St.
Kwun Chung Rd.
Bowring St.
Pilkem St.
Tak Shing St.
Austin Rd.
Austin Rd.
TST Police Station
Hillwood Rd.
TSIM SHA TSUI
KOWLOON PARK
Wing Lee Building
China Hong Kong City
Park Lane Shopper's Boulevard
Kimberley Rd.
Kimberley St.
Granville Rd.
Marco Polo Prince
Nathan Rd.
❷
❶
Burlington Arcade
Cameron Rd.
World Finance Towers
❸
Prat Ave.
Chatham Rd.
Ocean Galleries
Mosque
Humphrey's Ave.
Hart Ave.
Canton Rd.
Haiphong Rd.
Lock Rd.
Hanoi Rd.
Cornwall Ave.
Wing On Plaza
Kowloon
Ashley Rd.
Hankow Rd.
❾
❽
"Golden Mile"
Mody Rd.
❹
❺
DFS (Sun Plaza)/ Sun Arcade
Park Dr.
Shangri-La Hotel
HARBOUR CITY
Langham Hotel
Peking Rd.
Hyatt Regency -Hong Kong
Marco Polo Hong Kong
Metropole Building
Kowloon Hotel
❻
Far East Mansion
Middle Rd.
Tsim Sha Tsui Ⓜ
Ocean Terminal
Star House
Hong Kong Cultural Center
The Peninsula Hotel & Shopping Arcade
Salisbury Rd.
❼
HK Museum of Art
New World Centre
Promenade
⓬
Inter-Continental Hotel
Star Ferry To Central
Victoria Harbour

0   1/8 mile
0   100 meters

Museum 🏛
Transit Stop Ⓜ

Near Jordan Road, the atmosphere is more real. Be sure to get to the **Temple Street Market** (p. 130). And you can't miss the **Jade Market.** If you have a true spirit of shopping and adventure, you'll also make sure you get to Fa Yuen Street (see below).

HARBOUR CITY

Although it's technically part of Tsim Sha Tsui, I count the western portion of Kowloon as a separate neighborhood because it is basically one giant shopping mall, in the form of several huge interconnected malls. I call the whole entire stretch of Canton Road—from the Star Ferry to China Hong Kong City—Harbour City. This definition includes the buildings across the street on Canton Road, like **Silvercord** and the **Sun Plaza Arcade.**

The denser shopping is on the Ocean Terminal side, where (walking away from the Star Ferry) the buildings, in order, are: **Star House, Ocean Terminal, Ocean Galleries, Ocean Centre, Marco Polo Prince Hotel,** and **China Hong Kong City,** which is a mall-and-towers complex and ferry terminal. This entire stretch of shopping buildings also includes office space and residential towers, as well as some of the well-known tourist hotels in this area: Marco Polo Gateway, Marco Polo Hong Kong Hotel, and Marco Polo Prince Hotel.

TSIM SHA TSUI EAST

If you have Hong Kong Harbour at your back, Ocean Terminal to your left, and the InterContinental to your right, you're looking at the heart of Kowloon, or Tsim Sha Tsui. As the Kowloon peninsula curves around the harbor and the land juts away from Kowloon and the InterContinental, the area just east of Tsim Sha Tsui but before Hung Hom and the old airport is known as Tsim Sha Tsui East. Because it's waterfront property and just about on top of the KCR train station to China, it has a string of luxury hotels and a few shops.

Tsim Sha Tsui East fascinates me; I see it as a miniature version of greater Hong Kong. You can find almost everything you need right here. Mobbed on weekends by local shoppers, its various buildings include **Auto Plaza, Houston Centre,** and the enclosed mall itself, **Tsim Sha Tsui Centre.** There is street-level shopping all along Mody Road, in the various buildings, in the mall, and at street level of the buildings behind the Great Stafford and Nikko hotels. There is also some shopping in each hotel. My favorite store in this area is **DFS,** which has terrific souvenir, food, and traditional medicine departments.

YAU MA TEI

The most famous shopping site in the area is the well-known **Jade Market** at Kansu and Battery streets; look for the overpass of the highway, and you'll spot the market right below it. The experience is just short of mind-boggling. Here you can shop from 10am until 2:30pm, going from stall to stall, negotiating for all the jade (p. 127) that you might fancy. There are two tents filled with vendors. You'll never be strong enough to do both tents.

Alongside the Jade Market, on Shanghai Street, is a "wet market"—a real live Chinese **green market** (farmers' market) worthy of exploration with or without a camera. As the street stretches to the south, it has some old-fashioned paper stores.

At night you will want to visit the **Temple Street Market,** also in this district but not as far north as the Jade Market. As you push your way through the shoulder-to-shoulder crowds, you can buy from the carts, have your fortune told, or enjoy an open-air meal.

HUNG HOM

Home of Hong Kong's original outlets, this part of town will disappear once the real estate here goes up in value, due to the change in airports, scarcity of land, and opening of the new arts and culture center. Already the factory outlets here have gone downhill, and shopping visitors no longer feel compelled to visit. In fact, factories have already moved out, and the outlet scene is bad. If you have tons of time on your hands, maybe check it out. Most agree with me, though: Don't waste your time checking this out unless you are doing a dissertation on Hong Kong real estate.

The most famous address in Hung Hom is **Kaiser Estates,** an industrial development of factories and factory-outlet stores with a few fancy outlets—when you look at **JBH/Fashions of Seventh Avenue,** you'll be seeing a boutique as smart as anything in Central. There's no MTR stop; you'll need to take a taxi.

PRINCE EDWARD & FA YUEN

Even though Fa Yuen is just a street and not a true neighborhood, it's enough of an event that it should be considered a separate destination. It's my favorite new neighborhood in Hong Kong. On a recent visit, I bought so much I truly could not fit down the stairwell to the MTR station.

In a nutshell, Fa Yuen is the newer version of Granville Road. It's farther "uptown," deeper into the real Hong Kong, and a good bit cheaper than Granville Road, while offering much the same style of shopping—storefront after storefront of racks and bins filled with no-name and designer clothing for as little as $10 an item. Silk blouses cost a tad more, but not much.

Fa Yuen has been blossoming for several years now; no doubt it will become too commercial, and a new place will sprout. Until then, what are you waiting for? Bring plenty of cash because most of these stores do not take plastic. Consider bringing airline wheels—or a donkey. It is time to shop 'til you drop, Hong Kong style.

You must be prepared to rummage at Fa Yuen, but because you won't see guests from your hotel, you will feel like a real China hand for having come here and outsmarted everyone you know.

If you need a jumping-off place, head for **Come True,** 146 Fa Yuen St. Then there's **Kwong Shui Hong,** 190 Fa Yuen St.

Prince Edward, Mong Kok & Fa Yuen Street

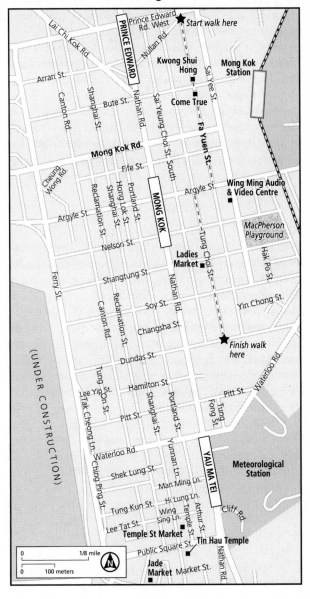

These 2 blocks are dense with great stores that sell overruns (mostly clothes) from the nearby factories; just walk from one to the next. They truly all look alike, but you'll be getting used to this kind of thing by now. Besides, after you've done Granville Road, this will come naturally to you. From here, you can wander over to the nearby **Ladies' Market** (see below). It's 2 blocks away on Tung Choi Street and opens around 4pm. Don't confuse these two shopping venues. This Ladies' Market is mostly a street market with stalls on the road, while Fa Yuen Street consists of traditional retail with actual shops. Look at a map. Also note that the **Bird Market** is in this neighborhood, on Yuen Po Street. To get there, take the MTR to Prince Edward.

MONG KOK

Mong Kok is having a huge image makeover with the arrival of its first luxury hotel, the **Langham Place,** which comes complete with designer shopping mall. This is a real-people part of town and great fun—it's filled with shopping ops. There's **Mong Kok Market** at Tung Choi Street, an afternoon market that is also called the **Ladies' Market** (see map). If you have evening plans and can't make it to the **Temple Street Market,** then Mong Kok is the afternoon market you should plan to visit. In addition to stands selling alarm clocks that cluck, blaring Canto-pop, and fake designer scarves, you'll find everything else you could ever need.

To get there: Depart the MTR at Mong Kok station and find Hong Lok Street, which is more of an alley, on the south side of Argyle Street. It's 2 blocks west of Nathan Road (if your back is to the harbor, then west is to your left).

Chapter Five

....

HONG KONG RESOURCES A TO Z

ANTIQUES

....

Hong Kong is home to many places to buy art and antiques. Two important things to remember:

- Internationally famous dealers do business in London, New York, Tokyo, Vancouver, Taipei, Brussels, and other places besides Hong Kong; buy according to reputation and trust, not location.
- The number of fakes and frauds in the art business is infamous and truly frightening, especially in Hong Kong.

Buy what you know; if you don't know much, buy what you love, regardless of its real value. Bring your own expert if you are truly serious, or hire one in Hong Kong. If you are considering something pricey, get a second opinion. Many dealers on Hollywood Road will appraise an item (from another source) for a flat fee.

Bear in mind that the truly wonderful pieces are usually put away. Most dealers have warehouses or back rooms where they keep their best wares; many are open only by appointment.

ARCH ANGEL
53–55 Hollywood Rd., Central (MTR: Central)

I can't tell you how many personal recommendations I have received from readers who love this source. Prices are high, but the name can be trusted. Open daily for furniture, statuary, and tabletop items. A second shop sells art.

HONEYCHURCH ANTIQUES
29 Hollywood Rd. (MTR: Central)

Honeychurch Antiques has been my home base on Hollywood Road since the beginning of the *Born to Shop* series; I know you will be well taken care of by American expat owners Glenn and Lucille Vessa. They have held court for over 25 years and know everything and everyone; stop by and ask whatever pops into your mind . . . but don't ask if you can call home.

The store carries a wide variety of merchandise. The look is sort of Oriental Country; there are goods from Japan and other exotic locations besides basic Chinese antiques. Try both floors in the main shop and a warehouse floor next door (ask to be taken over), with larger pieces of furniture and a few other goodies. Yes, they have blue-and-white; yes, they'll let you smell the opium pipes.

P.C. LU & SONS LTD.
Ocean Terminal, Harbour City, the Silk Road, Canton Rd., Kowloon (MTR: TST)

A fine antiques dealer with showrooms in the major hotels, P. C. Lu is owned by a family that has been in the business for four generations. It's one of the finest resources for antique ivory and jade, porcelain, and decorative work. The three sons who run the business work closely together. Stop in at any of the galleries and browse, or get a look when you're prowling the Silk Road.

ART

I try not to cover art in these pages because it is such a subjective thing. However, you will soon notice that Hong Kong—and a lot of the world—has gone bonkers for Vietnam's artists. (For information about shopping in Hanoi, see chapter 7.) One of the best Hong Kong galleries at which to see examples is **Arch Angel Art,** 38 Peel St., off Hollywood Road (© 852/2854-4255).

ARTS & CRAFTS

The Chinese look hasn't been so fashionable in years, certainly not since the Beatles took to wearing Mao jackets. Now everything's coming up ethnic, so Chinese classics are more chic than ever. You can buy them in markets, at souvenir shops, and at **Chinese Arts & Crafts,** the department store (p. 104). I have a few specialty sources.

KENKI
Bear Kingdom, Salisbury Rd., Kowloon (MTR: TST)

This store has a few other branches; I go to this one because of its location (between the InterConti and the Pen). It sells embroidered shirts and blouses, reversible silk-to-velvet or cotton and silk Chinese coolie shirts, brocade vests with and without fur, handbags, shoes, and an amazing selection of dramatic goods. Prices are excellent—about $40 for a shirt, $100 for an elaborately embroidered jacket.

X-QUISIT
Shop L141, Mall Place, InterContinental Hotel, Salisbury Rd., Kowloon (MTR: TST)

This store is behind the hotel's grand staircase and therefore may seem to be hiding from you. It also seems to have several names in the front window. The selection of crafted goods, from jewelry to notebooks, to hostess gifts, to robes, is very chic and very expensive. This is the kind of place that should be your first stop: You stare at and touch everything and then sigh.

RIBBON EMPORIUM
33A Haiphong Rd., Kowloon (MTR: TST), and other locations

I'm not sure which is funnier, the name of the store or my calling it a resource for arts and crafts. It's what many people would call a jobber and, despite the name, does not sell ribbon. But it does sell many arts and crafts items—from clothes to handbags to zip sacs—at unbeatable low prices. There are heaps of stuff everywhere. Not all of the stores are the same; there are several branches around town.

BATH PRODUCTS

See the "Spas" section (p. 141) for more information, and remember that this is a city where the InterContinental Hotel has a 24-hour "bath butler"—all sorts of beauty products for the tub (and shower) are readily available. For brands you may not be familiar with, high-tail it to any of the big malls.

One of the most popular imports is **Lush,** from England. There are some Lush stores in the U.S., but if you do not know the brand, this could be a good place to get acquainted. See "Cosmetics & Fragrances," below. The Canadian chain **Fruits & Passion** is similar to Body Shop when it first started out; it has branches in various malls, including Harbour City. I am also fond of Japanese bath salts. You can buy them in any drugstore or even grocery store and can somewhat tell the flavors by the pictures—since the package is entirely in Japanese.

BOOKS

Because English is still a second language in Hong Kong, it isn't hard to find books in English. True, they are pricey, but not as expensive as in other cities in China. If you need books for a long-haul flight or a cruise, this is the place to load up.

COSMOS
96 Nathan Rd., Kowloon (MTR: TST)

I stop in this bookstore because it is at the corner of Nathan Road and Granville Road, where I shop in the bins for closeouts. English-language books and stationery supplies are downstairs.

DYMOCKS
Star Ferry Terminal, Central (MTR: Central); IFC mall (MTR: Central)

There are a few branches of this store around town, but the most fun experience is to wander the small shop's aisles right before you board the ferry for Kowloon. You'll find international magazines, some stationery items, and plenty of fiction and nonfiction in English.

PAGEONE
Lower level, Times Square mall, Causeway Bay (MTR: Causeway Bay)

Branches of this small chain are often in malls alongside the grocery store City Super. Everything is in English, and the magazine selection is huge. There are a few nonbook items; the trophy of one of my sprees was an eight-lens camera for $50.

SWINDON BOOK CO. LTD.
13–15 Lock Rd. (behind the Peninsula Hotel), Tsim Sha Tsui, Kowloon (MTR: TST)

Although this medium-size store carries everything, the most impressive range is the selection of art books and books on Chinese culture.

CAMERAS

Forget it. Buy at home. And for heaven's sake, avoid those guys on Nathan Road. Okay, maybe that's not helpful. If you're talking serious money, buy at home.

If you're talking inexpensive, look around but don't get suckered. And please remember this little tale: I decided I needed a credit-card-size digital camera and tried to buy one for $59 on my flight from Hong Kong to Shanghai, but they were sold out. The same camera cost $149 on the flight from Hong Kong to Paris.

KING DRAGON
33 Mody Rd. (behind the Holiday Inn), Tsim Sha Tsui, Kowloon (MTR: TST)

This shop is for pros and those who know a lot about cameras. Ask for Alan.

CHAMPAGNE COURT
Off Granville Rd., Tsim Sha Tsui, Kowloon (MTR: TST)

This is a destination, not a single store. All of the dealers in this courtyard sell professional cameras to knowing photographers. They also carry many secondhand parts.

CASHMERE

....

Cashmere from the Orient is not of the same quality as that which comes out of Scotland or Italy because of how the yarn is combed and milled. Meanwhile, Iranian cashmere, which is of even lower quality than Chinese, is flooding the market. Price should be related to the ply number (from 1, the lowest quality, to 4); 2 is the usual number available in Hong Kong.

You can find cashmere in many of the outlet stores in the **Pedder Building,** in several different stores at the **Peninsula Hotel Shopping Arcade,** at **Stanley Market,** and even at the Chinese department stores. Quality will be a big issue here—it affects the hand (feel) as well as the price. Most likely, you can get cashmere at home for prices similar to those in Hong Kong. But wait, did I tell you about the **Tse Cashmere** outlet sale?

PEARLS AND CASHMERE
The Peninsula Hotel, Salisbury Rd., Kowloon (MTR: TST)

The selection of colors is excellent. Prices are not dirt cheap but are competitive with low-end prices in the U.S., meaning you get more quality than usual for the price, which is close to $200 per sweater. Some sweaters cost less; the store also carries other items.

TSE CASHMERE
Peninsula Hotel Shopping Arcade, Salisbury Rd., Kowloon (MTR: TST)

Tse (say "say") is a luxury brand with expensive merchandise sold at fancy stores around the world. Once a year, usually before Christmas, an outlet sale takes place at an address announced in the *South China Post* newspaper. When I went, the floor was dirty, but the merchandise (organized by size and color) was fabulous. The staff took credit cards and spoke English. Just about everything cost less than $100. It was a heart-stopping shopping moment, especially good for those who need luxury labels in their bargains.

CDs, VCDs & DVDs

··

CDs and **VCDs** (video compact discs) are sold on the street, in the usual music stores and chains (such as **HMV**), and in Shenzen.

Note that VCDs are not DVDs—DVDs are more expensive and are said to have better quality, although I have had no problem with the quality of VCDs. DVDs also hold more information, so a movie fits on one disc, as opposed to two (or more) VCDs.

The average price for a VCD in Hong Kong is HK$35 (US$4.50). However, when I last tested, VCDs did not play on a U.S. machine—though they do play on my U.S. laptop. New French players, even the cheapie ones that cost about $50, do play VCDs, so things might be changing in new machinery in the U.S., too.

I have yet to figure out whether some of the Kowloon sources for **DVDs** and VCDs are legal—they are so out in the open and so professional that they appear to be legal. Illegal DVDs are usually sold like copy watches: in back rooms, behind closed doors, on street corners. To help crack down on pirating, producers of legal DVD are lowering prices, so you can often get a legal DVD in the U.S. for $11 to $16. You may find this makes more sense than buying in Hong Kong, unless you know what will play on your home machine or computer.

On Nathan Road, off Nathan Road, and, in fact, in every neighborhood in Hong Kong, plenty of stores sell DVDs. Prices begin at $7 each. A boxed set of films or the entire season of a television show costs more. You'll find Chinese films, TV series, classic films, and more or less current films for sale.

You should also know the difference between the DVD-5 and DVD-9 formats; from my research, all I know is, if it doesn't say DVD-9 on it, don't buy it.

CERAMICS

··

Chinese crafts stores carry a selection of china. And yes, assume that blue-and-white is fake unless guaranteed otherwise.

OVERJOY
Kwai Hing Industrial Building, 10–18 Chun Pin St., Block B, 1st floor, Kwai Chung, New Territories (MTR: Kwai Hing, then taxi)

Located in the heart of Hong Kong's shipping and container district, where there are a few other porcelain showrooms, Overjoy is worth the trouble. Although it's not a replacement for the lost wonders of Wah Tung (see the next listing), it is a good source. The selection includes both Western and Chinese patterns. I bought ginger jars for $5, mugs with lids for $10, and lamps for $40. The store offers international shipping (rates are posted) and free delivery to Hong Kong hotels. There is also a showroom in Wan Chai. When you are ready to leave, the staff will give you a small piece of paper asking your taxi driver (in English and Chinese) to take you to the MTR station. Taxis are readily available out front.

WAH TUNG CHINA COMPANY
Wholesale showroom: Grand Marine Industrial Building, 3 Yue Fung St., Tin Wan, Aberdeen; call ahead

Stores: 57 Hollywood Rd. (MTR: Central); 8 Queen's Rd. East (MTR: Admiralty)

I have bad news for old China hands: Wah Tung, which for years was fabulous, has been sold. The selection is different (the new owners are pushing "European style") and the prices much higher. I've bought tons here in the past and loved every minute of it, but I am sorry to say that I don't feel the same now. The new shop on Queensway is walking distance from the Pacific Place mall but is otherwise in the middle of nowhere Wan Chai and, to me, not worth it. A coupon in *Where* magazine gets you 15% off your purchases. The retail stores have the same hours: 11am to 7pm daily. The factory is open Monday through Saturday 9am to 5pm. Take a taxi, but call first before schlepping out there to see whether the staff is expecting customers; they seem to be directing trade to their retail stores: © 852/ 2873-2272.

CHOPS

In China, a *chop* is a form of signature stamp on which a symbol for a person's name is carved. The chop is dipped in dry dye (not pressed onto an ink pad) and then placed on paper to create a signature stamp, much like a rubber stamp—though chops are not made of rubber.

Although chops vary in size, they are traditionally as big as a chess piece, with a square or round base. Up to four Chinese characters or three Western initials can be inscribed on the base.

Quality varies greatly, depending on the ability of the person who does the carving. We have done enough chop shopping to know that the very best place to get a chop, if you crave atmosphere, lies in **Man Wa Lane,** deep inside the Western District. It's also the worst place because it is so confusing— you may never find your way back to the proper vendor when you need to pick up your finished chop. Nevertheless, Man Wa feels very authentic, and you may enjoy the entire experience.

Every hotel has at least one gift shop that will have your chop engraved. Allow at least 24 hours. Many shops will provide 1-hour service. A variety of dealers at **Stanley Market** offer while-you-wait service.

You may buy the chop a la carte or in a set or gift box. The boxed set comes with your chop and the inkpot in a silk-covered (or faux silk) box with an adorable clasp; expect to pay about HK$100 (US$13) for a boxed set at Stanley Market.

COMPUTERS & ELECTRONICS

I am nervous about buying computers and most other electronics in Hong Kong—too much can go wrong. On the other hand, my greatest delight has been buying small DVD players to give as gifts in the U.S. They play DVDs, VCDs, and discs from all zones. Well, they play DVD-9 all over the world.

I shop for electronics at **Broadway,** a reputable chain with stores all over Hong Kong, and buy either the brands we all know or Shinco. Make sure the instructions are in English and that voltage is 110–220. You will also have to buy plugs. Another reliable chain is **Fortress,** which has stores in all trading areas. There are computer buildings, streets, and fairs (even a flea market) for locals who know what they are doing. Shop at your own risk.

BROADWAY
Times Square mall, 7th floor (MTR: Causeway Bay); 28 Soy St. (MTR: Mong Kok); and many other locations

I've had my share of bad experiences buying electronics in Hong Kong, so it's a pleasure to find a store I can trust. This is a chain with locations everywhere. I won't shop anywhere else.

FORTRESS
5 Peking Rd., Kowloon (MTR: TST), and many other locations

The other trusted name in electronics, with stores all over town. This one is behind the Pen. The downstairs (ground floor) area is smallish; go upstairs.

COSMETICS & FRAGRANCES

The best buys in this category are noteworthy in terms of availability, not price—check out scents that have been introduced in Europe but not in the U.S. Whether or not you save becomes meaningless because you'll be the first on your block to have the new scent. If you care. And I am not going to mention a brand just because it's new or hot in Hong Kong, such as Kiehl's (the latest thing), because you can easily get Kiehl's for less money in the U.S.

Many big-name cosmetics companies manufacture for the Far East in and around Hong Kong; often they will have a product with the same name as the one you use at home, but it will be slightly different. They may also have a product or shade that you have never heard of and will never find again anywhere else in the world.

If you just wander through any of the malls, especially **Harbour City,** you will finds tons of little shops selling brands that may interest you—a few local labels, some European brands that don't have good distribution in the U.S., and many Japanese products.

Designer Brands

MADINA
Shop 2412, Harbour City, Tsim Sha Tsui, Kowloon (MTR: TST); Times Square mall (MTR: Causeway Bay)

Those looking for something new, different, and not easily found at their local mall in the U.S. will love this line. Madina is an Italian makeup brand that is promoted as a slightly up-market mass-market brand—something for everyone. The *createur* of the brand is the makeup artist at La Scala opera house, and her husband owns the largest makeup factories in Italy, where many designer makeups are produced.

Prices on Madina are fair, and the colors are glorious.

Shu Uemura
*The Landmark, 16 Des Voeux Rd. (MTR: Central); Mall at
Pacific Place, 88 Queensway, Central (MTR: Admiralty);
Ocean Terminal, Kowloon (MTR: TST); and other locations*

Makeup junkies shouldn't miss the opportunity to buy from
the Japanese maven of cosmetics and color (although this line
is also available in the U.S. and Europe). There is even a kiosk
at the airport.

Mass-Market Opportunities

Bonjour
Locations all over town

This is a chain possibly devised for adolescent girls; I'm not
crazy for it, but your 12-year-old might enjoy it. It's a knock-
off of the SaSa concept (see below).

Boots
IFC mall, Central (MTR: Central)

Boots is a British chemist that sells several of its own brands
of makeup and treatments, among other things. Some Watson's
stores carry the line at in-store boutiques, but there is a growing trend toward freestanding stores for beauty items only (these
are not Boots stores as we know them in the U.K.), with an
emphasis on well-being products. The line No. 7—a riff on No.
5, as in Chanel—is an excellent color cosmetics selection at a
moderate price.

Jurlique
*Landmark Atrium, 16 Des Voeux Rd. (MTR: Central);
Times Square mall (MTR: Causeway Bay)*

Say "Jur-*leak*," then celebrate Australia and this terrific brand.
Lavender hand cream is the most famous of Jurlique's numerous products. I fly with Herbal Recovery Mist in my purse,

and I like the silk dust (instead of powder) for really sweaty summer days. The line is also sold at Faces, the beauty portion of Lane Crawford in Ocean Terminal, Kowloon. Prices may be lower in the U.S., but the line is not easy to find there.

LUSH
Shop 40, Festival Walk (MTR: Causeway Bay); Shop 3315, Harbour City (MTR:TST); Hong Kong International Airport, arrivals hall

You can almost smell a Lush shop before you see it; asthmatics need not apply. Despite the high prices, the British firm (which is spreading through the U.S.) is on to something charming. The deli-counter environment features beauty and bath products, soaps that are sliced like cheese, and bath bombs as large as tennis balls, ready to lob into a hot tub and make you giggle. The concepts and scents are the same throughout the world, but ingredients may be different in some international stores.

RED EARTH
Locations all over town

This Australian brand does color cosmetics and skin treatments. The moderate prices mean it's geared for a young customer.

SASA COSMETIC COMPANY
Locations all over town

SaSa has emerged as one of the leading discounters in Hong Kong, with branch stores everywhere. Note that all branches are not created equal; some have more stock than others.

Many goods come directly from sources in the U.S., which makes them much cheaper locally—but not cheaper than at home, if you are American. Shop carefully. Also note that some items are closeouts and discontinued lines.

WATSON'S, THE CHEMIST
24–28 Queen's Rd. (MTR: Central), and many other locations

There's a Watson's on almost every big, busy block and mall in Hong Kong; I stop in all of them because they're not all the same. Selected stores have a Boots department (see above). Watson's is actually a drugstore–cum–general store that sells many things, including other lines of makeup and treatments.

DEPARTMENT STORES

European-Style

HARVEY NICHOLS
The Landmark, 16 Des Voeux Rd. (MTR: Central)

Just when you thought the British had left Hong Kong, London's best department store arrives at the city's fanciest mall. Expected to be open by the end of 2005, the store will dance across five floors of the mall and will coordinate shopping ops with the new Mandarin Oriental Landmark, a boutique hotel in the mall.

LANE CRAWFORD
70 Queen's Rd. (MTR: Central); Mall at Pacific Place, 88 Queensway, Central (MTR: Admiralty); Times Square mall (MTR: Causeway Bay); IFC2 mall (MTR: Central)

Lane Crawford is the most prestigious Western-style department store in Hong Kong. It's a jewel to those who work and live here but crave the elegance of old-world charm in a retail setting. Lane Crawford is not huge by American standards, but you'll find all the familiar top-quality brands. It is not really for tourists, but it does offer the guarantee that you are not getting fakes, seconds, or inferior merchandise. Snobs often buy their jewelry and their lifestyle here. The newest branch, some 8,361 sq. m (90,000 sq. ft.) of razzle-dazzle, is in the IFC mall. Actually, I like the outlet store (p. 107) better.

LCX
Ocean Terminal, Harbour City, Tsim Sha Tsui, Kowloon (MTR: TST)

The concept is one big warehouse, so it's a department store within a mall—and one that has no walls. Brands have different identity areas, clearly delineated, but you wander from one to the next as if sailing from island to island. A few of them are names you know (Gap, Banana Republic), some are names you have been dying to meet, and others are totally unknown even to the savviest shopper. The space is young and hip, but it's also interesting if you just want to see something very different from an old-fashioned department store or mall.

MARKS & SPENCER
Harbour City Ocean Galleries, 25–27 Canton Rd., Kowloon (MTR: TST); Mall at Pacific Place, 88 Queensway, Central (MTR: Admiralty); the Landmark, 16 Des Voeux Rd. (MTR: Central); Cityplaza III, 1111 King's Rd., Quarry Bay (MTR: Tai Koo)

I love M&S, but there are no great bargains here. Being in the store, especially the grocery department, is just fun. It also offers a chance to buy Western sizes and larger sizes. Need a brassiere? Need shoes? Can't get a fit elsewhere? This is your source. Just watch out for clothes marked "Asian fit," which probably will not fit you. Women's shoes go up to size 42 (U.S. size 11).

Chinese

CHINESE ARTS & CRAFTS STORES (H.K.) LTD.
Flagship: Star House, next to Star Ferry, Canton Rd., Kowloon (MTR: TST); branches throughout town

This is the most Western of the Chinese department stores. By American standards, the prices are good, although the David Tang look-alike merchandise is just as expensive as his! Ouch! The stores are clean, easy to use, and tourist friendly, but you pay for these luxuries.

The silk-fabric (yard goods) department is fun, although the prices are cheaper in markets. I've been told this is a reputable place to buy jade. There's no imitation passed off as real here. *Be warned, however:* Real jade is quite pricey.

The store will ship for you; the sales help has been very pleasant to me—unusual for some Chinese stores. This is a good place for souvenirs. Hours in all stores are basically Monday to Saturday from 10am to 6:30pm; Sunday hours vary with the location.

Yue Hwa Chinese Products Emporium

Main store: 301–309 Nathan Rd., Yau Ma Tei, Kowloon (MTR: Jordan Rd.); also Park Lane Shopper's Blvd., 143–161 Nathan Rd., Kowloon (MTR: TST); and other locations

This is a real Chinese department store, with many convenient branches. Unfortunately, the newer the store, the more Western it is, which is not my favorite style of Chinese department store. Buy from the "Great Wall of China," as I call the china department; get silk pjs; get silk by the yard.

The main store is rather jam-packed and junky and absolutely divine. If this is too hard for your system to digest, the newer Park Lane store is almost as nice as Macy's. Ignore the Western goods and buy Chinese. The stores mail to the U.S. Hours are daily from 9:30 or 10am to 8 or 9pm.

Japanese

Most of the large Japanese department stores are in Causeway Bay and aren't very different from U.S. department stores. Seibu, the most upscale of all Japanese department stores, bucked the trend by opening in the Pacific Place mall. Hard times have forced cutbacks, but the store is still open.

SEIBU
The Mall at Pacific Place, 88 Queensway, Central (MTR: Admiralty)

Once one of the best department stores in the world, Seibu is now cutting back a tad. Perhaps the most interesting part of the store is the lower-level grocery store (p. 112), but the store still has many brands and strives to introduce brands that no one else has. The store likes to have the Belgian designers who get so much coverage in the fashion press but also has the first **Diesel StyleLab** in town.

DESIGNER GOODS

Hong Kong gains designer shops every day; I cannot come to town without being annoyed that so many new ones have opened. Who in the world is shopping at these places? Did any of us come to Hong Kong to buy big-name designer clothes at regular retail prices? Or to buy at prices higher than at home? I mean, *really*.

Every now and then you can get a break on designer goods, but not often. Some Chanel items (such as makeup) are cheaper than in the U.S. or at the airport duty-free shop. Most items, however, are not. If you are interested in a certain designer line, I suggest you shop for it at home and come to Hong Kong with notes in hand. Don't be surprised if designer prices are totally out of line; Ferragamo may just give you heart failure.

However, it is possible that you will find designer lines in Hong Kong that have not yet come to the U.S., or that you do not know . . . so you can be the first on your block to wear a certain style. Note that the stores seem to be staying in business because rich Chinese shoppers come over from the mainland.

Up-and-Coming Talent

More and more young designers are finding that Hong Kong is a fine place to be discovered. Although many of the young designers in town are not yet represented in boutiques, they are busy designing private-label goods for large stores. You may have never heard their names, but you may dig their designs.

You'll find the latest and wildest designs by hot young talents in the shops that line **Kimberley Road** and **Austin Avenue**. These two streets, in the northern end of Tsim Sha Tsui, have become the SoHo of Hong Kong. The shops' decor is avant-garde; the prices are affordable. Start at the corner of Austin and Nathan roads, walking east. Austin Road turns a corner and becomes Austin Avenue, which turns again and becomes Kimberley Road, heading back toward Nathan Road. Also in this area is the **Rise Commercial Building** on Granville Circuit, a small, hard-to-find alley off Granville Road.

DISCOUNT

Most manufacturing is done outside of Hong Kong, so there are few genuine factory outlets these days. Still, there are some jobbers in the **Pedder Building** (p. 120) and a handful of good sources elsewhere. Changes at **Horizons Plaza** make it worth the trip, and there's usually a line of taxis waiting to whisk you home—a recent improvement.

With the exception of Lok Wah, none of these establishments is near the MTR; take a taxi.

JOYCE WAREHOUSE
Horizons Plaza, 2 Li Wing St., 21st floor, Ap Lei Chau

Joyce has been the most famous name in European luxury brands in Hong Kong for over 25 years. She's had a number of stores and has suffered the usual ups and downs of retail in hard times. Her warehouse and outlet store sells off goods that don't move out of her stores. I saw an Armani blazer for $50 (U.S.!) and other designer bargains that left me breathless. Sizes tend to run small.

KAISER ESTATES
Phases 1, 2 & 3, Man Yue Rd., Hung Hom

This is a formerly famous shopping district that I find very boring and somewhat overpriced. A Donna Karan DKNY blazer for $250 is not my idea of a bargain. I did, however, luck into the Adidas outlet sale—shoes at $30 a pair were a good bargain. Most of the outlets are in Phase 1, with a few in Phase 2. Frankly, I think you can give this area a miss, but I got a note from readers who loved it here. Go figure.

LANE CRAWFORD WAREHOUSE
Horizons Plaza, 2 Li Wing St., 25th floor, Ap Lei Chau

Better than any Barneys outlet I've ever been to. Armani jackets for under $200; suits for $400. Shoes, accessories, home style, menswear. Gorgeous stuff. Maybe I got lucky, but it sure was more fun than the Joyce Warehouse.

LOK WAH
Lok Wah Bo, 193 Fa Yuen St. (MTR: Mong Kok); Lok Wah Top World, 175 Fa Yuen St. (MTR: Mong Kok); Lok Wah Top Place, 53 and 55 Granville Rd., Kowloon (MTR: TST); Lok Wah City, 11 Lee Garden Rd. (MTR: Causeway Bay)

This small chain of jobbers operates stores that sell clothes—often including big name brands—out of bins. Each major shopping area has a store, which can be your jumping-off point in its neighborhood. I'm not saying it's the best of the jobbers, but I have done well on repeat visits and found a variety of merchandise and sizes at low every-day prices.

SPACE
Marina Sq. E., 2F Commercial Block, South Horizons, Ap Lei Chau

Space is the name the Prada Group gives to its warehouses selling all its lines—Prada, Miu Miu, Jil Sander, Helmut Lang, and so on. With all the fake Prada in China, it's hard to suggest that you visit, but this *is* the real thing, and it carries clothes, shoes, and accessories, too. This outlet is in Ap Lei Chau but not in Horizons Plaza (though it is nearby). Ask your hotel concierge to call ☎ **852/2814-9576** for directions, then have him write them in Chinese.

ETHNIC STYLE

Costumey Chinese dresses, jackets, and shirts are for sale just about everywhere in Hong Kong, from souvenir stores to **Chinese Arts & Crafts,** to the chicest of them all, **Shanghai Tang** (p. 125). However, if you prefer the look that qualifies more as boho chic, you will need a good eye and some luck.

For one of my latest trips to Hong Kong and China, I spent $150 on an embroidered and quilted jacket from a bridge designer line. I found it in Hong Kong for $40. That is unusual, but it shows what can happen when you shop enough. The wares in most of the local arts and crafts stores will do the trick. Chunky beads, exotic fabrics, and layers of fashion can be found here and there; those with a good eye can piece them together.

FABRICS

As a rule, don't think that just because you are close to the silkworms, you can walk away with bargains. Silk is usually about $15 a meter.

Buying fabrics from tailors in the PRC can be tricky (they may lie about the origin of the goods), but you can trust the fine tailors in Hong Kong to offer European fabrics for suits, shirts, and other clothing. If you don't know your tailor, don't let him sell you European fabric without showing you the bolt or sample book. Low-class tailors have been known to do a switcheroo—or just fib.

The second floor of the Western Market (p. 130) is home to a fabric market. You may get a kick out of **Excellent Silk Mill**, 17 Cameron Rd., 2nd floor, Kowloon (MTR: TST), which takes only cash but has vintage fabrics for sale off the bolt. It's near Nathan and Granville roads.

Shanghai Tang sells gorgeous silks and fabrics, but the prices may kill you. For similar fabrics, try a branch of **Chinese Arts & Crafts.**

Shenzen, across the border (see chapter 6), is a good place to shop for silk. **Li Yuen West,** in the Lanes (p. 76), is more convenient.

FURS

Just when you thought it was safe to go out into the cold, fur is back. Fun fur—cheap, funky, colorful, and possibly fashion forward—is the latest trend and can be found in Hong Kong in the winter. There's also a far amount of fake fur around, even in markets. The most trusted name in real fur is **Siberian Furs** on Chatham Road in Kowloon.

GLASSES

The days of truly inexpensive eyeglasses are over, but many people do find considerable savings in Hong Kong.

EYE'N-I
1 Lan Fong Rd. (MTS: Causeway Bay)

With an optometrist in the shop and more designer frames than you can imagine, this is one of the hipper spots for eyewear in a very trendy neighborhood.

NEW FEI OPTICAL SUPPLY LTD.
Lucky Horse Industrial Building, 64 Tong Mi Rd., 1–7 Bute St., 12th floor, Kowloon (MTR: Prince Edward, then shuttle bus or taxi)

This source comes from my friend Louis, who is chief concierge at the InterConti and wears glasses (I had Lasik). Louis knows everything and everyone. And I wouldn't be telling you about this if I didn't think it was a winner.

So here's the deal. This is indeed a factory. You pick your frames, you have your eyes tested, and you wait 10 minutes. If your prescription is more complicated, you may wait a half-hour. You can buy reading glasses, eye glasses, or sunglasses prescriptions; children have their own selection. There are thousands of frames, many from big-name Euro designers. The eye test is free. The setup is sort of supermarket style, then you sit at a table with a mirror and try on frames all day. Cold drinks are served.

When I visited with my scout Mary, she had the test, chose the frames, and had her new glasses within a half-hour. She got progressive reading glasses in a chic French frame for $65. You can take the shuttle bus or a taxi from the MTR; the area is industrial but not frightening. To arrange for the shuttle bus before you head out, have a hotel staff member call © 852/2398-2088. Avoid weekends, if you can; some 400 people a day pass through on Saturday and Sunday. Hours are daily from 10:30am to 8pm.

GROCERY STORES

The best grocery stores in Hong Kong are more like department stores. Indeed, one of my favorite stores in town is called **City Super**—it sells everything. **Marks & Spencer** stores sell some packaged (not fresh) foodstuffs; the local grocery store chains, **Wellcome** and **Park 'N Shop,** have small branches all over.

CITY SUPER
Times Square mall (MTR: Causeway Bay); IFC2 Mall (MTR: Central); Ocean Terminal, Kowloon (MTR: TST)

I'm not sure if I am more in love with the wide selection of Japanese bath products, the gadgets department, the international foodstuffs, or simply the people who shop here—but this is a great business and a really fun concept. It's the modern version of the general store.

GrEAT
Mall at Pacific Place, 88 Queensway, Central, downstairs from Seibu (MTR: Admiralty)

I don't like GrEAT as much as City Super because it's more of a gourmet grocery and less of a department store. But baby, what a grocery store. There's a fancy food court and all sorts of international grocery and gourmet products. Branch stores are opening in Kowloon.

NEEDS
New World Centre, Salisbury Rd., Kowloon (MTR: TST)

Every time I check into the InterConti, next door, I make this my next stop. I'm not saying to make a special trip here (as I would suggest for any branch of City Super), but the Kmart-type establishment is a great grocery store. You can also buy health and beauty aids, electronics, and more.

SUPER WELLCOME
Causeway Bay (MTR: Causeway Bay)

Wellcome is a well-known grocery chain; this location is almost a superstore in the heart of crowded Causeway Bay, near the big hotels there. You can buy snacks and real-people needs, and browse in a fun, modern supermarket.

HANDBAGS

....

ASHNEIL
Far East Mansions, 5–6 Middle Rd., Shop 114 (up the stairs), Tsim Sha Tsui, Kowloon (MTR: TST)

As Ashneil himself says, "The quality has to be good; we have no logos."

These bags are not copies—they do not have designer logos or anything illegal. They just coincidentally look a lot like the handbags in the fashion magazines. These bags are not cheap, but they cost less than the designer versions. The company does private trunk shows across America, but you have to sign up to be invited while you are in Hong Kong. It is also possible to choose and pay for your bags in Hong Kong and have them sent from the U.S.—you save space in your luggage and don't worry about Customs or duties.

Ashneil is off Nathan Road a half-block from the InterConti, right behind the Sheraton. However, the building is what you might call funky, so first-timers may feel nervous. Don't be. Walk up one flight of stairs to the first floor and follow the signs to room 114.

MAYLIN
Peninsula Hotel Shopping Arcade, Salisbury Rd., Kowloon (MTR: TST)

If you are a regular here, note that the shop is in a different location on the same floor. If you aren't a regular, you must be on your first trip to Hong Kong. This is the best source for Birkin bags in strong fashion colors and reasonably priced (from around $300).

MERLINO
Kowloon Hotel, lower level B112, Kowloon (MTR: TST)

Merlino's basic Birkin goes for about $250, slightly less than Maylin's. Merlino also has a wider selection of styles and small leather goods. I buy fashion bags here, as well as wallets and gift items.

PENINSULA HOTEL PHARMACY
Basement, Peninsula Hotel, Salisbury Rd., Kowloon (MTR: TST)

Yeah, I know it's a pharmacy. It also sells Birkin and Kelly handbags. Priced by size, the bags cost $126 to $185, and less during occasional promotions. I have bought several bags here; my most recent was a black Birkin on sale. It is not the world's best Birkin—it does not compete with anything from Maylin, Merlino, or Ashneil—but the value for the money is excellent. For more information, e-mail: yakkyoku@hongkong.com. Shipping to the U.S. is available.

SAM WO
41–47 Queen's Rd., basement, Central (MTR: Central)

Sam Wo is an old source who has been on and off these pages for years. I am very conflicted about sending you here because it takes a very good eye in order to score. When I look at all the bags, they seem to jump off the wall and race toward me. I get dizzy, and the bags look cheap.

However, when I see a single bag worn by a stylish woman, I am always shocked when she tells me her treasure came from Sam Wo. For the same sort of thing, I like Shenzen better. If you can't get to Shenzen, you may have a ball here.

Expect to pay about $75 for a decent designer copy. The sales help claims to know nothing about the bags' hardware (metal trim). I know for a fact that they do have these items but are wary of arrest and so play dumb. You probably have to be a regular to get the extras.

Sam Wo has two shops: a tiny, stall-like location in the Lanes (p. 76) and a larger basement store, which has a door in the Lanes but an official Queen's Road address.

JADE

Books have been written on jade, and there is a small section in Chapter 3. The news here is that I now have a contact in the Jade Market, so you can ask for Erica and have her guide you to more honest dealers and help with your negotiations. She runs her business, **Jade Butterfly,** out of Booth #63. Her mobile phone, if you want to call from your hotel before you head over: © **852/9042-3872.**

JEWELRY & GEMSTONES

The jewelry and gemstone businesses are separate and converge only at the wholesale level, where you will never be admitted without a bona fide dealer. If you are serious about buying stones, you should be introduced to the wholesale dealers. This requires personal contact from a dealer in Hong Kong or from a friend who is Chinese and living in Hong Kong. It is a very tight business. Don't expect to just walk into a shop off the street and see the best stones or get the best prices.

There is risk in every purchase, but if you are dealing with a reputable jeweler, that risk is minimized. Reputation is everything. If you are looking for good pearls, diamonds, opals, jade, or ivory, educate yourself. Take the time to learn before you leap.

If you are into creating your own necklaces, you need to meet Jenny. You pick and buy the beads from her, tell her what you want, and she will string and deliver to your hotel. **Jenny Gems Company,** No. 364–65 and 410 Jade Market, Yaumatei (MTR: Jordan Road) or jennystore@hotmail.com.

The Good Stuff

GEMSLAND
The Mandarin Oriental Hotel, 5 Connaught Rd. (MTR: Central)

Richard Chen and his mother, Helen, run this family business; they carry many classic ready-made pieces suitable for their international clientele or will custom-make your order in 5 to 7 days. It's hard to give you an idea of price because it depends on what you have made. All the work they have done for me has been with unset gemstones I brought with me; I just paid $540 to have a ring made in 14-karat gold.

THE SHOWROOM
Central Building, Pedder St., 12th floor (MTR: Central)

I run with an expatriate crowd in Hong Kong that seems to do everything in groups; everyone knows everyone and shares the same resources. Many of those resources have become regulars in these pages. According to my sources, the place for jewelry these days is a small place simply called the Showroom, where a woman named Claire Wadsworth holds court. Good work at excellent prices is the general opinion, backed up by many I trust.

Not-So-Expensive Jewelry

ORIENTAL ARTS JEWELRY LTD.
ME9, mezzanine, Peninsula Hotel, Salisbury Rd., Kowloon (MTR: TST)

If you are into the ethnic chunky look, this store will leave you drooling. If you are a do-it-yourselfer, you can get ideas here and make a lot of this stuff yourself. Prices are not low, style is high, and the looks are downright stunning—but a lot of the basics can be found for less money in street markets. If you aren't the type to be bothered stringing and twisting and collecting and making it up, you will find semiprecious stones in necklaces, drops, earrings, and all that jazz.

PAN AM PEARLS
9 Lock Rd., Kowloon (MTR: TST)

I sometimes buy my faux pearls here, and I consider this is one of my single best sources in Hong Kong. The faux pearls I've bought here are about the best I've seen at these prices. I have seen fluctuations in quality according to stock, and I have yet to match the quality of the double-strand, 8-millimeter set that cost me $40 5 years ago. A strand of pearls runs about $20; the staff will string together several strands into a single necklace with a new clasp as you wait. Baroque pearls are also available.

LEATHER GOODS

Hong Kong is a big handbag and shoe destination for several reasons:

- If you go to Shenzen, you might buy a dozen handbags—fakes but also inspirations; see p. 149.
- Almost all American and European designer brands have shops in Hong Kong; you will find brands you've never heard of and models your neighbors haven't got.
- If you go for quality but don't need a brand name, you will be floored by the number of Kelly, Birkin, and Bollido bags in Hong Kong, usually in the $100-to-$300 price range. Hotel arcades (p. 124) are a good source for these items.
- The major malls and hotel shopping centers usually have stores representing European brands that often don't have distribution in the U.S. Check out **Nannini**, an Italian brand, in Ocean Centre or the Peninsula Hotel.

LOCAL HEROES

··

BLANC DE CHINE
Pedder Building, 12 Pedder St., Central (MTR: Central)

One of the best stores in Hong Kong: chic Chinese clothes for men and women, and home style.

GOD
48 Hollywood Rd. (MTR: Central); Hong Kong Hotel, 3rd floor, Kowloon (MTR: TST); Leighton Centre, Sharp St. East (MTR: Causeway Bay)

This store does not personify any deity; the name is an acronym for "Goods of Desire." It sells everything from furniture to soft furnishings, to home style. This is a great place for gift items.

JOYCE
2106 Canton Rd., Kowloon (MTR: TST)

Poor Joyce—the most brilliant and successful woman in Hong Kong retail has had her share of headaches with this nutsy economy. The store is just as eye-catching and fabulous as any other Joyce project. For information about the Joyce Warehouse in Ap Lei Chau, see p. 107.

KAI EN LO
Private showings only

This famous jeweler no longer keeps a shop but tours the world. Your concierge can contact her, and she will come to your hotel room.

WALTER MA
49A Kimberley Rd., Kowloon (MTR: TST)

Ma is in the category of designers who have been "up and coming" for 20 years. Nonetheless, his clothing is easy to wear and different from other brands that make you feel you look like everyone else. Much of it is for the young, but a lot of it is so imaginative that you have to grin.

MALLS

....

Hong Kong is totally overrun with shopping centers. It's as though a contagious disease has spread to all architects, who now feel compelled to equip hotels and office buildings with three floors of retail shops.

Central

IFC2
1 Harbourview St. (MTR: Central)

This is the new tallest building in town, the location of the new Four Seasons Hotel and the home of a very nice mall, complete with a **City Super.** There's also cinema, an MTR station, and an Airport Express stop as well as a great view to Kowloon. Just about every major store has a branch here; Lane Crawford's new flagship is here.

THE LANDMARK
16 Des Voeux Rd. (MTR: Central)

The most famous of the Central malls, the Landmark has the reputation and the big names in luxury retail, and it stays ahead of the game by adding new stores and concepts. The latest innovations are a Mandarin Oriental boutique hotel and the first Asian branch of the London department store Harvey Nichols.

I suggest this mall as a jumping-off place for Westerners who want to see something but aren't quite ready for Kowloon. After a quick survey, you'll probably find that everything is gorgeous but very expensive, and that you are ready to move on. There are a few cafes here for lunch.

THE MALL AT PACIFIC PLACE
88 Queensway, Central (MTR: Admiralty)

If you are staying in one of the many hotels built next to the mall, this place is a natural for you. If you are in a hurry, you may want to come by because you can pack a lot in.

Note that the official name of this place is the Mall at Pacific Place, but everyone calls it **Pacific Place.** Technically speaking, Pacific Place includes the office tower above the mall and the fancy hotels grouped around the tower (Marriott, Conrad, Island Shangri-La).

PEDDER BUILDING
12 Pedder St. (MTR: Central)

Well, the Pedder Building is looking downright spiffy. My bet is that rents have risen, which explains why almost all the old favorites have moved out. Although it's across the street from the **Landmark,** it offers the opposite in shopping appeal—outlet stores on one side and the famed **Shanghai Tang** at street level. Most of the outlets in the Pedder Building have dried up, but you might want to poke around and see. There are two reliable destinations: **Shopper's Safari** and **Blanc de Chine.** Note that Blanc de Chine is not discount or inexpensive or anything other than Armani with an Oriental twist.

PRINCE'S BUILDING
Chater Rd. (MTR: Central)

This office building with five levels of shopping has so many big names now that it competes with the **Landmark** and the **Central Building,** both of which are across the street. The Prince's Building connects by bridge to the Mandarin Oriental Hotel (don't miss shopping there, either) and may be more fun than the Landmark. It is not mind-boggling like the Landmark, so you can shop and enjoy yourself, and it houses many other big names in international deluxe brands.

Causeway Bay

FASHION WALK
Gloucester Rd., Causeway Bay (MTR: Causeway Bay)

Not technically a mall, Fashion Walk is a shopping concept. The street level of several adjacent buildings—three of them in sort of a triangle—houses up-and-coming designers, cutting-edge designers, Japanese designers, hopeful designers, and the likes of Vivienne Tam. There are also several cafes. On the Victoria Park side of the Excelsior Hotel, this destination is extremely refreshing because the stores are unique and you aren't inside a mall too much of the time.

LEE GARDENS 1 & 2
Leighton Centre and Hennessy Centre, 111 Leighton Rd. (MTR: Causeway Bay)

This mall has so many fancy designer shops that you'll forget you are in Causeway Bay. The two buildings lie perpendicular to each other: Lee Gardens 1 is on Hysan Avenue, and Lee Gardens 2 is between Yun Ping Road and Jardine's Crescent. The two malls have brands such as Chanel, Hermès, Vuitton, Paul Smith, Prada, Cartier, Longchamp, Gucci, Bottega Veneta, and so forth. You get the picture. Philippe Starck designed the new Jean-Paul Gaultier shop.

TIMES SQUARE
1 Matheson Rd. (MTR: Causeway Bay)

The mall is divided by category of goods, which simplifies life for someone shopping for a specific item; it combines Western chains and big names with local dealers and small firms. There are four floors of restaurants. This is a destination, not merely a mall, and it attracts a lot of young people. My favorite shop is **City Super,** a grocery store and department store in one (enter through Lane Crawford).

Aberdeen

HORIZONS PLAZA
2 Lee Wing St., Ap Lei Chau (no nearby MTR)

This is not a mall, but it functions like one. The high-rise tower houses many furniture showrooms, wholesale sources, outlet stores, carpet stores, and gift sources. It's worth the trip because of the selection.

The **Joyce Warehouse** is in this building; I've never done well with Joyce in outlet stores, but hey, you never know. The **Lane Crawford** outlet is here; I found it great. **Tequila Kola** is sort of a large version of Pier 1 Imports: It carries tabletop accessories, bed linen, curtains, and small decorative items, but it's known for furniture. That makes it more of a source for locals—unless you want to ship (which you can) or are just looking for ideas. The large space holds a number of room sets. The tenants change frequently, but there are so many of them that you can still have fun. Each store keeps its own hours. There's a free directory at the welcome desk. Taxis wait out front.

Kowloon

HARBOUR CITY
Canton Rd., Kowloon (MTR: TST)

The shopping complex that occupies most of Tsim Sha Tsui's western shore is generally known as Harbour City. It includes **Ocean Terminal, Ocean Centre,** and **Ocean Galleries** along with the **Hong Kong Hotel,** the **Marco Polo Hotel,** and the **Prince Hotel.** There are four levels of shopping, and if you can successfully negotiate your way from end to end, you won't even have to come up for air. All luxury brands have stores here, as do most chains.

NEW WORLD CENTRE
18–24 Salisbury Rd., Kowloon (MTR: TST)

The New World Centre is yet another massive, multilevel, spic-and-span, concrete-and-cold-floor shopping center filled with little shops, 1-hour photo stands, and ice cream vendors. It has a cute Japanese department store (**Tokyu**—open Fri–Wed 10am–9pm) at street level, but really, don't waste your time on my account. If you are a guest at the adjoining InterConti— or any nearby hotel—the grocery store (**Needs**) is a lot of fun and sells all sorts of things besides groceries.

PARK LANE SHOPPER'S BOULEVARD
Nathan Rd., Kowloon (MTR: TST)

This architecturally unique strip mall will certainly catch your eye (and maybe your credit card) as you stroll the infamous Nathan Road. **Yue Hwa**, a Chinese department store, occupies about half of the space. There's also an **American Express.**

Mong Kok

LANGHAM PLACE
8 Argyle St. (MTR: Mong Kok)

With 300 stores, this is the hot new place in town for the younger crowd, as well as an attempt by the city to rejuvenate the area. Part of the mall is the snazzy new Langham Place Hotel. There are also the usual cineplex and food court. This mall is not a destination for tourists, so it's a great place to get a look at the future—Mong Kok is arriving, the young people from China are arriving, and the trendy clothes and concepts are already here. And it's not at all down-market or funky: There's a branch of the posh Japanese department store **Seibu** as well as a huge branch of **Muji.**

Hotel Arcades/Hotel Malls

The fanciest hotels have the most trustworthy shops. Certainly the shops in the **Peninsula** are the most expensive and most exclusive. But that doesn't mean there's anything wrong with the shops in the **Holiday Inn,** which happen to be touristy but fine if you want a TT (tourist trap). And get a look at what's going on underneath the **Kowloon Hotel:** You'll find some big names like **Tommy Hilfiger** as well as the **Jurlique Day Spa.**

THE INTERCONTINENTAL HOTEL
18 Salisbury Rd., Kowloon (MTR: TST)

As the hotel arcade/shopping center/mall sweepstakes heats up, this small mall offers one of every big name (including **Chanel**) *and* adjoins the New World Centre. This is not a destination mall but a convenience for hotel guests. More interesting is the new **Shanghai Tang** in the hotel lobby.

KOWLOON HOTEL
19–21 Nathan Rd., Kowloon (MTR: TST)

A small, underground arcade you reach by escalator directly from the street. There are two levels of basement stores, all small but uncrowded. Because of its association with the Peninsula Hotel, the hotel has a classy retail arcade with big-name designer tenants.

THE MANDARIN ORIENTAL HOTEL
5 Connaught Rd. (MTR: Central)

The glitziest stores in town fight for space in the Mandarin Oriental, not only because the hotel is so fabulous and its clientele so tony, but because the location is prime. Part of your Central shopping spree must include a visit to the stores here, which include **Ferragamo, Fendi, David's Shirts,** and **Gemsland,** my jeweler. The Mandarin Oriental also has one of the best hotel gift shops in the world—not the news kiosk on the lobby floor, but the store marked GIFTS & FLOWERS in the shopping arcade (SH on the elevator panel).

THE PENINSULA HOTEL
Salisbury Rd., Kowloon (MTR: TST)

Small shops fill the eastern and western wings of the hotel, with more on the mezzanine and still more in the basement. Every big name in the world has a shop here.

Also here are a branch of **Shanghai Tang,** several cashmere shops, and several leather-goods shops that make handbags and shoes. If you ever want to go into Kelly-bag overload, step this way. The glitzy modern pharmacy in the basement overflows with Western and Chinese goods, European perfume brands, and more handbags. (It also fills local prescriptions.) The Pen has its own store, too.

MARKETS

Markets offer a real slice of life and one of the few less-than-glamorous looks at the real China. Some are not pretty or fancy. If you are squeamish, avoid the food markets that sell live chickens or ducks and slaughter them on the spot.

Merchandise markets are busy and hectic. Each has its own clientele and its own personality. There are no spacious aisles or racks of organized clothing. Some markets exist only at certain hours of the day or night. At a preappointed time, people appear from nowhere, pushing carts laden with merchandise. They set up shop along the street and sell their goods until the crowds start to dissipate, at which time they disappear into the night.

Most markets have no specific street address, but are known by the streets that bound them or that intersect in the middle of the market area. Most cab drivers know where the markets are by name. However, it is always a good idea to have your concierge write the name of the market and location in Chinese.

You probably won't need it, but it can't hurt. Buses, trolleys, and the MTR usually serve the markets as well. Take a hotel business card with you so you'll have the address in Chinese. The following markets are open daily.

BIRD MARKET
Yuen Po St. Bird Garden, next to the Mong Kok stadium (MTR: Prince Edward)

The Bird Market is really just an alley that sells birds and bird supplies, but it's also an experience you will never forget. The sound of the chirping is overwhelming. I just want to know if the noise is made by birds chirping or grasshoppers chirping. The vendors sell bird supplies (including grasshoppers); you will be surprised at how many bird cages you suddenly want. You won't buy much here, but it is fun.

CAT STREET MARKET
Cat St., just below Hollywood Rd. (MTR: Central)

Cat Street Market is Hong Kong's answer to a flea market: Vendors sell used merchandise of the tag-sale variety from blankets and a few stalls on a 2-block stretch of pedestrian pavement just below Hollywood Road. One guy sells only used typewriters and used sewing machines. A few dealers sell old jade, which I like. One vendor has Chinese sunglasses from the 1930s. The shops behind and around the market specialize in formal antiques; some of these stores are reputable and even famous.

FA YUEN MARKET (FLOWER MARKET)
Fa Yuen St., Kowloon (MTR: Prince Edward)

This is not the Ladies' Market, although the two very different markets are close enough to be a single destination. For walking directions, see p. 87. Some people call this the Flower Market only because a few vendors sell fruit and flowers in baskets. A nearby flower market sells flowers, plants, and plastic greenery. You're here for the fun fashions, however, and will be walking toward Argyle Street. With Prince Edward to your rear, walk toward Kowloon.

The jobbers on Fa Yuen Street (p. 87) are open during the day when the market is closed. But at about 4pm, the street becomes a pedestrian mall, filled with fruits and veggies, handbags and brassieres. The jobbers remain open, so this is a mad case of too many bins, not enough money.

You will not see many tourists in these parts; the rummaging through bins may not be to everyone's liking. This is my favorite kind of shopping, and I always find deals. You'll see men's, women's and children's clothing as well as plus sizes in various jobbers' stores on both sides of Fa Yuen running for about 3 blocks. Cash only. ATMs are not that easy to find, so be prepared.

JADE MARKET
Kansu and Battery sts., Yau Ma Tei, Kowloon (MTR: Jordan Rd. and walk a bit or take a taxi)

The market is in two freestanding tents under the highway overpass at Kansu and Battery streets.

The Jade Market is an official market organized by the Hong Kong and Kowloon Jade Merchants Workers' and Hawkers' Union Association. Each merchant inside the fence is licensed to sell jade and should display his or her license above the stall. It is a good idea when buying to note the number next to your purchase, just in case you have a problem later on and the jade turns out to be plastic.

If you are not willing to bargain here, don't buy. The merchants in the Jade Market expect to lower their price by 20% to 40%, depending on your bargaining skill and their need to sell. Market hours are 10am to 3pm, although many of the vendors close up at 2pm. Go early rather than late.

LADIES' MARKET (MONG KOK MARKET)
Argyle St. and Nathan Rd. (MTR: Mong Kok)

The market sets up a short distance away from the Mong Kok MTR station; it begins around 4pm and goes into the evening, until about 10pm or so. It really gets going after work and seems to be a date spot. Watch your handbag.

The streets have the feeling of a carnival, with lots of people parading by the stands, stopping to examine shirts, socks, sewing sets, buttons, and bras. There are some toys and sunglasses—mostly lots of trinkets, clothing, everyday goods, and the usual ringing alarm clocks, fake designer goods, electrical doodads that flash and whirr—no live snakes or chickens. It's very different from Fa Yuen Street, so visit them both, if at all possible.

THE LANES
Li Yuen East and Li Yuen West, Central (MTR: Central)

The Lanes are twin alleys, about 50m (164 ft.) apart from each other, darting between Queens Road and Des Voeux Road in Central. I had given up on them for several years, but a friend asked me to reconsider for this revision. I had a ball. Furthermore, the women I took here all liked it a lot.

The general layout of each lane is the same—stores along the thoroughfare, and a center aisle of stalls. One lane specializes in Chinese arts and crafts, T-shirts, fabric off the bolt, and blinking electronic toys that make annoying sounds. This is also a good place for reading glasses that fold up into a slim tube.

The other lane specializes in handbags and padded bras. (Could I make this up?) Bra Lane also has several jobbers; I personally have never met a jobber I could walk past. On my last foray, I bought a pair of Nautica khakis for $10 and a T-shirt for $4. There is also a branch of the **Ribbon Emporium** (p. 92), that crazy source. *Hint:* It doesn't sell ribbons.

The stores and stalls are crowded and active; you are pestered and pursued and pressured to buy. Haggle till dusk.

Who need a trip to mainland China when you can shop here? Also note that this is an excellent neighborhood to snoop around in—1 block from Shanghai Tang and the Landmark, yet in another world. Queen's Road has many branches of favorite stores, even the Chinese department store **Yue Hwa**. And there are lots of banks with ATMs.

LUEN WO MARKET
Luen Wo, New Territories (KCR from TST East to Fanling, then bus no. 78 or taxi)

This is an authentic local food market quite near the border with China. The market and the merchandise are not enormously different from what you'd see in town, so the trip may not be worth your time. On the other hand, if you crave a peek into the real China or a world gone by, this is your Sunday adventure. The market fills a square city block. The shoppers are far more rural-looking than those you might find in downtown Central. You go here for the total experience, for the fact that it's real. You might want to give it a miss if there have been avian flu outbreaks.

STANLEY MARKET
Stanley Main St., Stanley Village, Hong Kong (public transit: bus no. 6 from Exchange Sq. in Central or no. 20 from Star Ferry)

Any tourist coming to Hong Kong knows about Stanley: Shopping legends abound about bargains in this village-cum-market-cum–tourist trap. Some people love Stanley; they are mostly first-timers. Stanley has become so touristy that I can barely cope—and I go there often, just to make sure I am up-to-date. I found no retail stock and no fake designer merchandise (oh, woe!). All I found were tourist goods—white linens, Chinese pajamas, knickknacks, and cheap gifts. Not bad if you want that sort of thing, but I wanted deals. Actually, I bought three "van Gogh" oil paintings for $6.50 each. The market is open daily from 10am to 7pm. A taxi will cost about $15 each way; the bus from Star Ferry takes about an hour.

TEMPLE STREET MARKET
Temple St. and Jordan Rd., Kowloon (MTR: Jordan Rd.)

This night market has grown a lot over the years, and as it spreads, the charm is diluted, making it yet just another street market. You have to know where the Chinese opera singers and the fortune-tellers are in order to find them.

Exit the MTR onto Nathan Road toward **Yue Hwa Chinese Products Emporium.** You will see Yue Hwa; you can't miss it. Stay on the Yue Hwa side of the street (this is still Nathan Rd.). With the harbor to your back, it's the left side. Walk north on Nathan Road for 2 or 3 blocks. Keep looking to your left. You are searching for a tiny entranceway, a small alley crammed with people. This is where the opera singers do their thing on little patios. When you spot the alley, turn left into the crowd.

This alley is only about 45m (148 ft.) long. When you emerge from the alley, you will be on Temple Street, at the corner of a real temple. Walk forward 1 block, keeping the sidewalk that borders the grounds of the temple yard on your right side. On this sidewalk you'll see a long row of fortune tellers, each with his (they're all men) own gimmick. One or two may speak English. The market itself begins thereafter.

WESTERN MARKET
323 Des Voeux Rd., Central (MTR: Sheung Wan)

Once upon a time, Western Market was a dump. Then along came a developer who turned the space into a festival market. It has a branch of **Fook Ming Tong,** the fancy tea broker; there are toy soldiers and plenty for kids to see and buy. Many of the cloth merchants who were disenfranchised when Cloth Alley was destroyed have taken space on the second floor of Western Market. Flags fly, banners flap, people shop. The space has a lot of energy and a number of unique stalls that sell merchandise I haven't seen anywhere else in town. True to its name, this market is much farther west than the rest of Central's basic shopping areas.

MEN'S SHIRTS: MADE-TO-MEASURE

There are a lot of choices to be made: the fit of the body, the type of collar and cuffs, the fabric, and the possible use of contrast fabric. Prices usually depend on the fabric: 100% cotton costs more than a poly blend; Sea Island cotton costs more than regular cotton. Expect to pay about $75 for a Sea Island custom-made cotton shirt, although such a shirt can cost more, depending on the maker. For custom shirts, two fittings are necessary—one for the measurements and one with the garment.

Many shirt houses have a minimum order; most tailors make shirts as well as suits. If you are buying the shirt and the suit from the same tailor, there is usually no minimum shirt order. Most shirt houses also make pajamas and boxer shorts.

ASCOT CHANG CO. LTD.
The Peninsula Hotel, Salisbury Rd., Kowloon (MTR: TST); InterContinental Hotel, 18 Salisbury Rd., Kowloon (MTR: TST); Prince's Building, Chater Rd. (MTR: Central)

Perhaps the best known of the internationally famous shirt dealers, Ascot Chang advertises heavily in the U.S. and stresses its quality and devotion to fit. This shirt maker has many branches in Hong Kong and Kowloon. The shops are filled with wonderful fabrics imported from Switzerland and France. Prices are competitive with **David's** (see below); mail order is available once your measurements have been taken. Shirts run between $40 and $125, depending upon the fabric and style. Top of the line. Ascot Chang also has a shop in Manhattan.

DAVID'S SHIRTS

Victoria Hotel, Unit 201, Shun Tak Centre (MTR: Sheung Wan); Mandarin Oriental Hotel, 5 Connaught Rd. (MTR: Central); Wing Lee Building, 33 Kimberley Rd., ground floor, Kowloon (MTR: TST)

David's is the other most popular of the custom shirt shops in Hong Kong. It's less glitzy than **Ascot Chang** (see above) but just as famous to those in the know. David's also has a branch in New York City. The main shop in Hong Kong is in Kowloon, on Kimberley Road. But there are more convenient branches, mostly in hotels like the Regent and the Mandarin Oriental.

David's will copy any shirt you like; just bring it with you and plan to leave it. The shop also has a framed illustration of collar and cuff styles you can choose from. Mail order is not only possible, but common with repeat customers. If you cannot get to Hong Kong, ask for a current swatch and price list. Return a shirt that fits you perfectly and a check, along with fabric and collar and cuff choices. Approximately 4 to 6 weeks later, a box of new shirts will arrive.

MEN'S SUITS: MADE-TO-MEASURE

Probably the most famous Hong Kong fantasy is that made-to-measure suits grow on trees or that they are easily and inexpensively obtained with a snap of the fingers and a few hundred dollars. No way. Remember the first law of Hong Kong custom-made suits: A bargain is not a bargain if it doesn't fit. Furthermore, the whole point of a bespoke suit is psychological—you must feel (and look) like a king in it. Its impact derives from the fact that it was made for your body, that it moves with you as no off-the-rack garment can.

- Start your search for a tailor the minute you arrive. Leave yourself time for three fittings while in Hong Kong. The first will be for measurements and choice of fabrics; the second will involve a partially finished suit with only one sleeve in place; the third will be to detail the finished garment. Good tailors usually have everything wrapped up by the third fitting.

- If at all possible, choose your tailor before you leave home and fax ahead for an appointment so you can meet shortly after arrival in Hong Kong. For the two best men's tailors in Hong Kong, see below. After you check in to your hotel, the tailor should be your first stop. You may want to choose your hotel based on the convenience to your tailor.

- Most tailors carry a full line of imported fabrics from Italy, England, and France. If your tailor is not one of the top two, ask whether the thread is imported also. If it is not, ask to see the quality, and test it for durability. Remember all those horror stories you have heard about suits falling apart? It wasn't the fabric; it was the thread. You do not need to worry about quality at the two biggies.

- Well-made suits from a Hong Kong tailor are not inexpensive. Imported fabrics run about $20 to $80 per yard, and an average-size suit will take 3½ yards. Silk-wool blends and cashmeres cost more. The finished price for a top-quality, killer suit runs $550 to $800. You could do better in some cases with an off-the-rack suit in the U.S., but the quality would not be the same. Your suit should be the equal of a $3,000 Savile Row suit.

- The tailor will want a 50% deposit to start the work. You may be able to pay with a check in U.S. dollars or pounds sterling. Ask ahead of time.

- If you are having the tailor ship the suits to you, remember to figure in the Customs charges and shipping. On average, air freight costs $20 per suit. Shirts can be shipped for $30 per dozen. U.S. Customs charges about $75 in duty on a single new suit. Once you have established an account with a tailor or a shirt maker and he or she has your measurements on file, you can simply get fabric swatches sent to you and do your shopping through the mail—or in a local hotel, if your tailor visits major U.S. cities.

- Check to see if the tailor you have chosen travels to the U.S. to visit customers. Chances are, if you live in a major city (New York, Washington, San Francisco, Los Angeles, or Chicago), he or she will. Most of the tailors I recommend either come in person once a year or send a representative with fabric books and order forms. At that time, new measurements can be taken in case you have lost or gained weight.

The Big Names: Hong Kong's Finest Tailors

A-MAN HING CHEONG CO. LTD.
Mandarin Oriental Hotel, 5 Connaught Rd. (MTR: Central)

Fondly referred to as "Ah-men," this shop turns out quite a few garments for the rich-tourist-and-businessman trade and, therefore, has become adept at relating to the European-cut suit. The tailors don't even blink twice when you ask for an extra pair of trousers. They just smile and ask for more money. The prices here are on the higher side, with a suit beginning around $650.

A-Man will also do custom shirts for approximately $50 to $150. © **852/2522-3336**; fax 852/2523-4707.

W. W. CHAN & SONS TAILOR LTD.
Burlington House, 92–94 Nathan Rd., 2nd floor, Kowloon (MTR: TST)

Peter Chan carries on a family business, which he has built and expanded over the years. He also has two shops in Shanghai (p. 216). The average price for a suit is $650 to $800; mink-cashmere blends can cost more. The W. W. Chan showroom is decidedly more relaxed than other big-time contenders' spaces. The showroom is neat, clean, modern, and even spacious, which is hard to find in Hong Kong. But the location in Kowloon and the approach to the actual showroom are not so swank; businessmen who are used to wall-to-wall carpet may need a moment to adjust. © **852/2366-2634.**

PASHMINA

Although solid-color pashmina shawls are sort of dead as a fashion statement, there's some leeway for those who want to beat the chill in the air stylishly.

FINE N' RHINE
Lyton Building, 42 Mody Rd., 3rd floor, Kowloon (MTR: TST)

This store sells handbags and some jewelry and accessories, but you want to ask to see the locked pashmina room, where all sorts of beaded, printed, and stylized treasures await. Also baby pashmina for the next grandchild.

PEARLS

If you are searching for pearls and pearls alone, you have many options. Every jewelry store has them in the window. The question is: Whom do you trust?

The value of a really good pearl is based on size, color, and evenness. More important, it's based on the number of layers of nacre. The untrained eye cannot see the layers of nacre and cannot guess if a pearl has only a layer or two that will quickly wear off with use. That's why you go to a reputable jeweler.

The bigger jewelry shops are safe bets for quality pearls. The price tag will be higher than on the street, but you have some assurance that, should you have a problem with your second appraisal back home, the shop will make amends.

Remember that part of the value of the pearls is based on color and that different cultures prize different colors. Different women may prefer differing shades of pearls to complement their skin tone. I happen to like my pearls on the pink side; most prefer their pearls very white. The English like their pearls to be creamy.

The size of the pearls and the length of the strand are other factors in price; if the strand has graduated pearls (in varying sizes), it will probably cost less than a strand with pearls of all the same size. To check on the uniformity of the size of the pearls, roll the strand with your palms and fingertips along the black velvet mat provided by the jeweler. You'll feel every bump and inconsistency.

The clasp is usually sold separately from the pearls for two reasons:

- Pearls without a clasp enter the U.S. with less duty, making this an attractive product to many Americans;
- The clasp is essentially a piece of jewelry and can cost as much as or more than the pearls, depending on size and the inclusion of gemstones.

Negotiating for the clasp (or a change of clasps) on any given strand or strands of pearls should be a separate piece of business from buying the pearls.

To help you get ready for your pearl purchase, you may want to contact **Tiffany & Co.** (© 800/526-0649; www.tiffany.com), which publishes a free brochure on buying pearls.

RESALE

This is somewhat of a new category in Hong Kong (and Kowloon). It follows a major trend in London, Paris, and New York: Many socialites take their year-old designer clothes and accessories to resale shops, which sell them to the public for less than full cost. Ah, the consummate Hong Kong Hobson's choice: to buy used or fake? Used is more expensive.

AMIE/THIRD AVE. LTD.
Pedder Building, 12 Pedder St., 3rd floor (MTR: Central)

This resale shop stocks clothes as well as handbags and some shoes.

FRANCE STATION
80 Russell St. (MTR: Causeway Bay)

Heads up—this will be on the final. The resale shops related to the next listing (Paris Station) are all named after cities, so Milan Station is part of that family. This store, however, is part of a different group, with a name chosen to confuse or blend with the concept. This store's main specialty is designer bags.

PARIS STATION
Metropole Building, 12 Hankow Rd., Kowloon (MTR: TST)

This is one shop in a growing chain—other stores have names such as Milan Station and so on. Paris Station sells designer handbags and accessories. It's around the corner from the Kowloon Hotel and behind the Pen, so you're going to be in the area anyway. There are no bargains, but it's fun to poke around. For information about the newest shops, call © 852/ 8200-7588.

VIP STATION
61 Granville Rd. (MTR: TST East)

I think this is a third chain getting into the action—its business cards list another store near Times Square. I like this one because after you've been bin shopping at the jobbers on Granville Road, it's fun to finish up here. Mostly designer handbags in good condition, but pricey.

SEX TOYS

This is a relatively new subject for this book, but someone asked me to make a purchase for her, so here's what I've learned. Of all the Asian destinations, Hong Kong is one of the most prudish, and finding a sex district (where is Suzie Wong when you need her?) or silly shop was not easy. Finally, at **Temple Street Night Market** in Kowloon, I found what I was looking for—several vendors selling vibrators of all sorts. Batteries included. Demonstrations free. Oh, my.

SHOES

Cheapie

There is an entire district of inexpensive shoes in the neighborhood known as Happy Valley, but it's a schlep, and large feet need not apply. Fa Yuen Street, which has many other shopper's delights, also has inexpensive fashion shoes—yes, shoes for $20 a pair.

Custom

LIII
Shop 75, Tower 2, Admiralty Center, 18 Harcourt Rd. (MTR: Admiralty)

This store used to be called Laces, and it was inexpensive. Now it's LIII (*L* with a Roman numeral). The staff sells shoes, copies shoes, and makes shoes with your own fabric. But it's not truly cheap—expect to pay over $100.

Designer Names

ANYA HINDMARCH
Mall at Pacific Place, 88 Queensway, Central (MTR: Admiralty); Lee Gardens (MTR: Causeway Bay)

First known for handbags, this British big name now sells shoes in the oh-la-la category.

JIMMY CHOO
The Landmark (MTR: Central)

Now that *Sex and the City* is off the air, you can trade in your Manolos for Jimmy Choos. Who can tell the difference, anyway?

Kate Spade
Mall at Pacific Place, 88 Queensway, Central (MTR: Admiralty); Harbour City, Kowloon (MTR: TST); IFC mall (MTR: Central)

Located in the major malls, Spade sells handbags, shoes and some home accessories.

Large Sizes

If you wear an American women's size 10 or larger, you may have trouble finding shoes in Hong Kong. In a shoe emergency, head to Marks & Spencer, which carries up to size 42 (American size 11).

Sports

Inexpensive sports shoes are readily available in all markets. They may or may not be counterfeit. Stanley Market is a little easier to shop than Fa Yuen's night market, but prices will be better on Fa Yuen Street in Mong Kok.

SOUVENIRS

It's not hard to find gifts or souvenirs in Hong Kong—they are everywhere. Actually giving the gifts to your friends will be harder; I always want to keep everything for myself. I included some gift suggestions in chapter 1. Below are a few stores that specifically sell great gifts.

City Super
Times Square mall, Causeway Bay (MTR: Causeway Bay); Harbour City, Kowloon (MTR: TST); IFC2 mall (MTR: Central)

I listed City Super under "Grocery Stores," but it is really a department store of goodies with a complete section of dry goods separate from the foodstuffs. Tons of inexpensive novelty items—especially beauty supplies and bath items—make great souvenirs and gifts. I bought many in packaging that I could not even understand.

DFS (DUTY FREE SHOPPERS)
DFS Galleria at Sun Plaza, 28 Canton Rd., Kowloon (MTR: TST); DFS Galleria at Chinachem Plaza, 77 Mody Rd. (MTR: TST East)

This is a department store meant mostly for Japanese shoppers but handy to all. I don't like it for normal designer shopping only because it bores me. When it comes to souvenirs, however, DFS may have the best in town.

A department in each store sells Chinese meds, foods, and souvenirs—I'd head there, ignoring the Burberry and Chanel. Don't miss the keychains, including one that allows you to insert your own photo into the body of a Chinese warlord.

DFS sells in bulk units, with prices discounted according to how much you buy. It has shuttle bus service that makes a loop from a few major hotels to the stores, and will deliver your purchases to your hotel so you can continue shopping with free hands.

MANDARIN ORIENTAL FLOWER SHOP
Mandarin Oriental Hotel, 5 Connaught Rd., Central (MTR: Central)

I am not sure how to account for the name; this is one of the best hotel *gift* shops I have ever seen. Note that it's not the ground-floor shop, but a store in the shopping mall on the mezzanine. If you shop a lot in Hong Kong, you will recognize that a lot of the merchandise comes from Wah Tung and other local sources for porcelain; a lot of it also comes from Vietnam. Prices are higher than they would be if you went out and found this stuff. But you're paying for the good eye of the buyer and the fact that everything in this shop is stunning and at your fingertips.

SPAS

....

Most of the swank hotels in Hong Kong have had spas for quite some time, and they have all refurbished their spas to take on the competition. Especially with the problems caused by jet lag—or the general need for detoxification—a trip here is no longer complete without some sort of treatment.

Note: All of the spas listed in this section require a reservation. Most hotels let nonguests test the spa waters.

The latest trend is foot treatments. Hawkers on the street will hand you brochures or try to lure you into alleys for a treatment. One of the nicest evenings I spent in town was an early dinner with friends and then a trip (for all four of us) to a foot spa.

ACUPRESSURE & MASSAGE CENTRE OF THE BLIND
Dragon Seed Building, 39 Queen's Rd., 7th floor, Central (MTR: Central)

My husband used a blind massage therapist and swore by her. Now you can try out the concept—and at very fair prices. The 1-hour treatments cost about $40. © **852/2810-6666.**

CLARINS AT THE PENINSULA
Salisbury Rd., Kowloon (MTR: TST)

I arrived at the Pen half dead and can truly say this was one of the first times in my years of treatments that I could really notice a difference. The energy massage began with a careful personal history, then a discussion of my health and needs, then a steamy shower with aromatherapy products. The 1-hour treatment cost just under $100; I added a tip for a job well done. I wasn't a hotel guest that time; when I am, I book the spa and the airport transfer at the same time. Last visit, I opted for a jet-lag treatment. © **852/2315-3271.**

I-SPA
InterContinental Hotel, 18 Salisbury Rd., 3rd floor, Tsim Sha Tsui, Kowloon (MTR: TST)

Not to be confused with the E-Spa brand of spa products, I-spa will cure whatever else ails you.

I always do a spa treatment after my long-haul flight and tried "Ancient Rituals of the Orient" recently. It was amazing, right down to the part when my neck and arms were stretched against tension and sprung free from their pins and needles and jet-lag woes. The treatment was so successful in helping me get acclimated to local time that I also booked a treatment for my evening of departure.

This time I did a face treatment that actually aerated my skin. It wasn't so relaxing, but it was therapeutic. I could see the difference immediately after the treatment and felt it was a smart thing to do before spending 12 hours in a tin can flying across the world. © 852/2721-1211, ext. 81.

PLATEAU
Grand Hyatt Hotel, 1 Harbour Rd. (MTR: Wan Chai)

This new addition includes a 23-room section of the hotel, as well as the city's most incredible spa. © 852/2588-1234.

Foot Spas/Reflexology

Foot spas are everywhere. I am always reluctant to try just any old place (I am still Dr. Kalter's daughter), so the ones I list here were suggested by friends and tested by my tootsies. Wherever you go, if there is no disinfectant process as you begin, grab your shoes walk out.

BIG BUCKET FOOT
Shops 1 and 2, Hoi Kung Court, 264 Gloucester Rd. (MTR: Causeway Bay)

I will always have a soft spot for this place, my first foot spa, because I first thought it was a shoe store for large sizes. It's half a block from the Excelsior Hotel and not too swish—but it is clean. Your feet soak in a big bucket, hence the name. The 90-minute treatment costs about $20; I tipped HK$20 ($2.60) afterward. I did a treatment before leaving for the airport on departure eve and swear it helped me. © **852/2572-8611.**

HENG LAM FONG
Star House, 3 Salisbury Rd., 18th floor, Kowloon (MTR: TST)

When I told Louis, the chief concierge at the InterConti, that I was researching reputable foot and reflexology treatments, he suggested this establishment. Located right at the Star Ferry, it provides traditional Chinese medicine as well as reflexology and massage treatments. The staff's English can be spotty. © **852/2376-3648.**

TAI PAN FOOT SOAKED BATH
18 Middle Rd., Tsim Sha Tsui, Kowloon (MTR: TST)

This is one of the fancy, clean, and swank places, as befits its address right behind the Pen. You take off your shoes and socks and put them in a locker, soak your feet to disinfect them, and then settle into a first-class airline seat for a treatment that will have you floating. Prices begin at $20. © **852/2301-3820.**

TEA

Some of the best tea in China is sold in Hong Kong. In fact, it's sold everywhere, and it makes a great gift. The packaging seems to be the main attraction—to me, anyway—but there are many tastes you won't find at home, and they're far more exotic than Lipton Yellow Label. Not that I'm knocking Lipton. If you do not know the Yellow Label line, which I don't think is sold in the U.S., you might want to try it. It makes excellent iced tea.

The listings below include individual brands and retail chains. Don't forget that every supermarket has a large selection.

BOJENMI
Chinese supermarkets such as Needs, New World Centre, Kowloon (MTR: TST)

The red-and-white Bojenmi brand box has an illustration of a girl playing the lute. I find that the tea smells like dead fish and tastes worse. But I have several friends in Hong Kong who swear by it. They claim you get used to it and then eventually like it, and that in 6 months, the cholesterol numbers will drop and life will be much more healthy. So I am doing my three cups a day. But I am nursing the same teabag through the three cups because it tastes better when it's weak.

CHINESE HEALING TEA
Locations in major MTR concourses, including TST (near exit B), Central (exit A), and Admiralty MTR (exit A)

About a dozen of these little shops—all clean and white and spiffy—operate in MTR stations. They're selling their packaging, their hype, and their marketing skills. The shops have tea, jellied tea, and a line of health products made from tea. You can taste brewed teas. I can't tell you whether any of the teas work, but for $10 you can get a cute gift package.

FOOK MING TONG
Western Market, 323 Des Voeux Rd., Central (MTR: Sheung Wan); Ocean Terminal, Harbour City, Tsim Sha Tsui, Kowloon (MTR: TST); IFC mall (MTR: Central); and many other locations

This is the leading chain of tourist-oriented (excuse me) tea shops, selling tea and teapots. The shops are adorable, the selection is exotic, and there is nothing too unusual about it. The packaging is so perfect that you will be comfortable and willing to buy all your gifts here.

YING KEE TEA CO.
151 Queen's Rd. Central (MTR: Central); Shop G8, 28 Hankow Rd., TST, Kowloon (MTR: TST); and other locations

This is a small chain with a store in just about every major shopping district in Hong Kong.

TEENS & TWEENS

All of Causeway Bay—the area behind the Excelsior Hotel and between Times Square mall and Lee Gardens—is a hive of teen, tween, young, and hip fashion. It's mobbed but exhilarating. Try to avoid the hours when the kids get off work in the evenings, unless you want to observe the phenom rather than shop.

THE ALLEY
New Territories. MTR: Lai Chi Kok

A garmento friend from the U.S. brought me here—I never would have found it on my own! It's possible that "The Alley" is the name given to it by Americans who work this space looking for hot new ideas—there are no signs that say THE ALLEY. Do we care? This is a trade building with a ground-level floor filled with stall after stall of shops selling teen and tween fashions at *grrreat* prices. It's an amazing social phenom just to be here and watch it going on swirling around you, but it's not for princesses. You walk down a center aisle that gives you the feeling of being in an alley, hence the name. It is indoors; it is truly incredible.

To get there, take the B2 exit from the MTR, walk away from the green and yellow towers, and turn right at the Hong Kong Industrial Center. Enter through parts B/C.

SUN ARCADE
78 Canton Rd., Kowloon (MTR: TST)

This small mall is underground, as is the fashion—which is mostly Japanese. Sizes are small, but the clothes are so fabulous that creativity freaks will be drooling. The crowds are also fun. Located beneath DFS.

WATCHES

....

As they say on the street, "Copy watch, lady?" Indeed, you can buy a fake Rolex or save money on a real Rolex. The trick is finding the right watch at the right price. You can pay anything from $50 to $10,000 and still not know what you have bought. Furthermore, the savings seem to be on high-end merchandise, so, yes, you can save $3,000 on a $15,000 Rolex—but did you really want a $15,000 Rolex in the first place?

Some things to be aware of before you buy:

- Check to see that the whole watch and not just the movement was made by the manufacturer. A common practice in Hong Kong is to sell a Swiss watch face and movement with a Hong Kong–made bracelet. The bracelet is probably silver with gold plating. This can work to your advantage if you do not want to spend $5,000 for a solid-gold watch but want the look. A reputable dealer will tell you that this is what you are buying and will price the watch accordingly. These watches cost $150 to $400.
- Check the serial number on the inside movement against the serial number on your guarantee.
- If you do not receive a worldwide guarantee, don't buy the watch.
- Do the same careful checking at brand-name dealers that you would do at a no-name shop. We know of someone who bought a brand-name watch from a reputable dealer, got the watch home, and had problems. When she turned to

the brand's U.S. dealer, she learned that, yes, indeed, she had bought one of their watches, but the movement was 5 years old. She had bought a current body with a used movement!

If you are simply looking for something unusual and fun, try **City Chain,** a huge chain with a branch in every mall and shopping district. It carries Seiko, Bulova, and Zenith, among other name brands, as well as fashion watches like Smash (a takeoff of Swatch).

Copy watches are sold in every market and on the streets of Nathan Road. Far better copies are for sale in Shenzen, although quality varies and the whole process can be overwhelming. Expect a Triple-A quality (the best fake possible) version of a Cartier watch to cost about $150. Prices for watches in Shenzen begin at $10.

WOMEN'S CLOTHING: MADE-TO-MEASURE
....

I started going to **W. W. Chan** for the simple reason that Peter Chan made my husband's clothes. Of the top two tailors, only W. W. Chan has a women's division.

Women are charged a flat rate for the making of the garment (no matter what size or how complicated); you pay for the fabric by the yard or provide your own. A woman's suit totals about $750, depending on the fabric. French wools (the same ones used at Chanel, and so on) bring the cost up. A dress costs about $170 for labor alone; a jacket, $175. See p. 134 for the W. W. Chan address and coordinates. To make an appointment or send a message directly to Danny Chen, who makes my clothes, write danny@wwchan.com.

Chapter Six

···················

PEARL RIVER DELTA: SHENZEN, CANTON & MACAU

WELCOME TO THE PRD

··

You can get a small taste of China with a day trip, overnight visit, or weekend in the nearby Pearl River Delta, or PRD. This is one of the fastest-growing areas in China, and once you really get into it, you can participate in the new China. The main shopping cities are Shenzen, Canton (Guangzhou, sometimes spelled Quangzhou), and Macau; they encircle Hong Kong. The entire area is part of the Guangdong Province. Do not confuse Guangzhou (say "gwan-joe"), the city, with Guangdong, the province.

With Hong Kong as your base, you can do a circle tour, plan a series of days out or nights away, or even arrive through one of the area's flashy new airports—which often offer less expensive flights than those that go direct to Hong Kong. All sorts of adventures are out there, waiting for those who dare to do something a little bit different.

Local Lingo

Once you cross into China, you can expect the ability to speak or understand English to plummet. One morning I asked for "two eggs, poached" and got two eggs, toast. They sound amazingly similar when you think about it. Learn to speak Chinese or get a grip.

Tourist Guides

Because very few American tourists go into the PRD, few tourist guides cover the area. For specific information, often in Chinese and English (very helpful when dealing with taxi drivers), check bookstores in Hong Kong, which carry several locally printed guidebooks. Shop carefully—many guides are out of date.

WELCOME TO SHENZEN
....

I've seen Shenzen described as "the new Hong Kong," which sort of puts Shanghai in an awkward position. To me, Shenzen is the new Shenzen. It is a fishing village with no history and no locals, as well as a get-rich-quick scheme that has gone mad with success. Although Shenzen has a theme park and many destinations-cum-attractions for Chinese locals, Shenzen is mostly a shopping destination or day trip for tourists staying in Hong Kong.

For those not doing business here, Shenzen (say *Shum*-sum in Cantonese) is actually a visit to one building—a sort of giant mall where the merchants take Hong Kong dollars and you barely know you are in China. As the focus of a shopper's day trip, this is a destination for fake designer merchandise. If you have more time, you can spend the night, see some of the local wonders (such as Wal-Mart), and enjoy the low-cost beauty services.

The day trip to Shenzen is as good as a trip to the far side of the moon, but I have to say right up front that I do not condone fake merchandise. For the most part, I think you get what you pay for—fake is fake. It won't last, it usually looks cheap, and it tarnishes your reputation.

In the years that I have been doing this day trip, it has gotten somewhat easier—there are now signs in English. The new train station makes it possible to jump onboard right in front of the InterContinental Hotel in Kowloon, and, vroom vroom—you are soon walking across the border into China. If you're making Shenzen an overnight or weekend destination, you have a choice of several international hotel chains, including a new Hilton.

Serious Shopper Notes

Consider taking a rolling suitcase for all your purchases. Wear comfortable shoes. Wimps and wusses need not apply. Have plenty of cash and patience. Prices are in Hong Kong dollars, not yuan—although if you use a cash machine in Shenzen to make a withdrawal, you will receive yuan. And speaking of cash machines, there are stories of scams galore, such as gangsters following people to the ATM and forcing them to withdraw big bucks, and stores saying they take credit cards and taking a card "to the bank" but really making copies of it.

To be safe, remember:

- Deal only in Hong Kong dollars and cash that you have brought with you, secured in a safe place.
- Do not follow anyone up a flight of stairs or into an alley to a secret source for designer fakes or for pirated DVDs.
- Shop with a buddy when possible.

Rush Hour

Stores in Shenzen don't open (in the Mall, anyway) until 10am, giving you plenty of time to arrive. Allow 1 hour from Kowloon to the mall. Rush hour is 7 to 9am heading inbound, and 5 to 8pm heading outbound. Try to leave Shenzen by 4pm if you are on a day trip.

Avoid holidays, Fridays, and weekends.

Shenzen

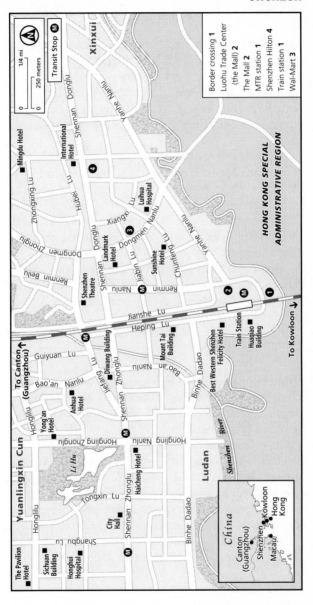

Border crossing **1**
Luohu Trade Center
(the Mall) **2**
The Mall **2**
MTR station **1**
Shenzhen Hilton **4**
Train station **1**
Wal-Mart **3**

HONG KONG SPECIAL
ADMINISTRATIVE REGION

Transit Stop 🅜

0   1/4 mi
0   250 meters

Xinxui

Mingdu Hotel

Zhongxing Lu

International
Hotel

Shennan Donglu

Yanhe Nanlu

Hubei Lu

Luihua
Hospital

Xiangxi Lu

Dongmen Nanlu

Dongmen Zhonglu

Xiangxi

Dongmen Zhonglu

Renmin Belu

Landmark
Hotel

Shenzhen
Theatre

Dongmen

Jiabin Lu

Sunshine
Hotel

Chunfeng Lu

Yanhe Nanlu

Nanlu

Renmin

🅜

Jianshe Lu

Heping Lu

To Canton
(Guangzhou) ↑

Guiyuan Lu

Jiefang Diwang Building

Mount Tai
Building

Train Station

Best Western Shenzhen
Felicity Hotel

Huaqiao
Building

To Kowloon →

Bao'an Nanlu

🅜

Shennan Zhonglu

Bao'an
Nanlu

Binhe Dadao

Anhua
Hotel

Yong'an
Hotel

Honglu

Hongling Zhonglu

Hongling Nanlu

Hongling Nanlu

Shenzhen River

Ludan

Li Hu

Haicheng Hotel

Yuanlingxin Cun

Honglilu

Tongxin Lu

Shennan Zhonglu

Binhe Dadao

City
Hall

🅜

Shangha Lu

Honghui
Hospital

Sichuan
Building

The Pavilion
Hotel

China
Canton
(Guangzhou)
Shenzhen
Kowloon
Hong
Kong
Macau

Spend the Night

A day trip to Shenzen is an amazing experience: It's power shopping to the max, and it will leave you exhausted but giggling. You'll sink into your hotel spa with a whimper and wake up the next day mad at yourself for not buying more. The experience is easier if you stay overnight. You can avoid rush hour traffic, and you have a chance to get a grip on your mental health.

I had always done this excursion as a day trip until this revision, when I spent the night at the new Shenzen Hilton. I found the major advantage of an overnight was the lack of pressure when shopping in the Mall. I probably stayed there the same amount of time, but I didn't feel pressured or frazzled. When I went back the next day, I was a more confident and better shopper.

It was a far better adventure to spend the night, dine at the Hilton, have my feet rubbed, drink Great Wall wine, and pretend I knew something about the new China.

Getting There

BY TRAIN

From Hong Kong, take the brand-new KCR train from East Tsim Sha Tsui in Kowloon. The train costs HK$36 ($5) for regular service and HK$72 ($9.35) for first class, which consists of a reserved seat.

Rush hours are crowded; at other times, standard service is fine and you should get a seat. The train is easy to use and well marked. The place to stand while awaiting the first-class compartment is designated on the platform.

Trains leave so often that you don't need a schedule or a reservation—buy a ticket and wait for the next train. Get off at the last stop, Lo Wu, and follow the crowds. The ride is 34km (about 21 miles) and takes about a half-hour.

By Bus

Citybus Express Coach offers bus service to Shenzen; there is transfer service at the border. In Hong Kong, call © 852/2736-3888 for more information, or ask your hotel concierge.

Formalities

Because you are crossing the border into mainland China, it's not a breeze. Also note that due to the current political situation, the rules are in flux. As we go to press, U.K. and U.S. passport holders may not get visas at the border. You can get a visa in Hong Kong within 24 hours—your hotel concierge will charge approximately $150 for 24-hour service and a $50 service charge. There are less expensive ways to do it, but they aren't as easy. See "Getting a Visa" on p. 18 for more information.

Once you have the visa, this is the drill:

1. Get off the train at Lo Wu. You are now in the New Territories. Exit the Separate Administrative Region (SAR) by going through the formalities here.
2. Walk into a second building and officially enter China with more paperwork and your visa.
3. Walk across a bridge, and you are in China.
4. Go up the stairs in front of you, and you are 100m (328 ft.) from the Mall.

Going back, it's the same thing. Allow about 1 hour each way for the formalities; it can take 3 hours. It can also take 30 minutes, but that's rare.

Getting Around

Shenzen is quite large and has many neighborhoods. If you are just going to the Mall, you will walk and never learn more.

Those who are staying or exploring can get a taxi in the train station or hop into the new Metro. In one stop, you are at the Hilton.

The Mall shopping district is not downtown, but in a commercial strip near the border crossing that is designated in addresses as Lo Wu district. Most of the international hotels are in this area also, although you may not want to walk if you have a lot of bags or luggage.

Note that streets and buildings are not usually marked in English, although this is changing and the big shopping buildings closest to the border now have signs you can read. Once you get oriented, so to speak, you will not need to read much—but you may find that my inability to give you more specific addresses is annoying until you get used to the lay of the land.

Taxis are cheap, but don't expect your driver to speak English. Have all destinations written in Chinese and in hand.

Calling Around

Shenzen is in China and uses the 86 country code. The city code is 0755.

The Lay of the Land

The main drag, an enormous, wide highway with low-slung modern commercial centers in long strips, is called "Sino-British Street." It's technically in Shatoujiao, the area east of downtown—and leading right from the Shenzen River and the Customs House. This street may be written as "Jia Dian" or "Jian She" in pinyin. Most streets have a direction after the name—for example, Shennan Road East, Shennan Road Central, Renmin Road South, Renmin Road North.

This highway is lined with commercial centers and malls. Some have individual shops inside, and many just have stalls or tables or tiny selling areas. These malls have names like Shenzen Commercial Center or Lo Wu Commercial Center and are hard to tell apart. They all offer four or five floors of selling space, with floors joined by escalators. There's usually a restaurant on each floor and toilets (have tissues on hand).

The more real part of Shenzen is called East Gate, which also appears on some maps as East Gate Business Pedestrian street. This is one Metro stop away from the Mall, at the far edge of Lo Wu District.

Money Matters

If you are just shopping in the Mall, you pay in Hong Kong dollars. In all other parts of Shenzen, you use Chinese currency, yuan (also called RMB). There are some 15 offices of major international banks in Shenzen, as well as scads of ATMs.

The Mall

Luohu Trade Center, better known simply as the Mall, is five stories high, connected by escalators. There are restaurants and toilets on all floors. The Mall sells just about everything. I go mostly for gifts, and I do load up. The floors are more or less organized by categories of goods, but these are not a rule—so you will find jewelry on other floors and not just in the jewelry mart, and so forth.

The designer copy handbags are often in the ceiling hidden from police because there are constant crackdowns on fake merchandise. They cost $75 to $100 and rival the ones I bought in Hong Kong for $250.

Note that a "fake" has a logo on it, and an "inspiration" of a classic is a style without any attempt to fake the hardware or logo—such as bags inspired by the Birkin and Kelly styles. Inspirations are 100% legal. Some copies, especially in watches, are graded by quality. A triple-A (top) rated Cartier-style watch can cost $150 after hard negotiating. A cheapie Chanel copy watch may cost $15.

There is a fabric mart and a row of tailor shops, although it takes several visits to have garments made, making this impractical for the day-tripper. The better shops are on the fourth floor.

The merchandise available in the Mall very much depends on fashion trends and police crackdowns. On my last trip, the latest fad was JPTod's shoes, which were selling for about $12 a pair. Fake fur handbags were hot; Prada merchandise was scarce. Franck Muller watches were "in"; Cartier watches are classics. Many stores had stacks of robin's egg blue boxes (fake Tiffany & Co.). There were fake Hermès ties and scarves, some in fake orange boxes. Most of the fake stuff does not look or feel real.

East Gate

Not far from the Mall, perhaps a 20-minute walk or zippy subway ride (one stop), you are in East Gate, the part of Shenzen where locals shop. There is a night market on a pedestrian street with a scene common to all major Chinese cities and fascinating for a first glimpse—the young people are out to spend their money and consume. Stores sell fashion, phones, DVDs, and electronics. The clothes won't fit you and the brands are possibly fake, but it's fabulous fun to observe the scene.

Sleeping in Shenzen

HILTON SHENZEN
2002 Jiabin Rd., Lo Wu District, Shenzen

This is a modern hotel, originally built as something other than a Hilton, so it might not be in your guidebooks. It has a terrific spa. Several restaurants offer many styles of cooking; a buffet is in a restaurant that revolves around the hotel tower, offering views of the city and off to Hong Kong. The breakfast buffet has both Western and Asian breakfast tables; you can ignore the chicken feet, if you want. Aside from all this, you stay here because it's a Hilton and the staff knows how to take care of foreigners.

The location is also sensational. The hotel is walking distance to Wal-Mart and to many branches of Starbucks; it's across the street from the local branch of Seibu, the famous department store chain (this one is a miss), and half a block from two luxury shopping malls. The Metro station is also half a block away. There's a branch of Bank of China across the street. The concierge will give you a good map of the city plus a taxi card with a map printed on one side. U.S. reservations © 800/HILTONS. Local © 755/2518-5888. www.shenzhen. hilton.com.

WELCOME TO CANTON
....

Canton is one of those famous names in trade and shopping that seems to stick, long after it has been replaced by the politically correct Guangzhou. Canton was one of the original 19th-century treaty ports and has been a center of commerce ever since. Now it stands midway between Shenzen and Macau in the circular loop of the PRD. It is headquarters for those who are adopting a Chinese child (the U.S. consulate is here), home of the most famous trade fair in China, and one of the most exciting cities in the new China. I am not easily overwhelmed, but I admit it, Guangzhou intimidated me. This is not a day trip from Hong Kong (if you can help it) and can be a lot more raw than the other trips in this area suggested in this chapter.

Why Canton?

I asked myself this question the entire time I was there. I had a fabulous visit, my hotel was great, and I did buy some terrific items. But it's a hard trip—mostly because of the language difficulties, not because of the lack of Western lifestyle—and not for everyone. If you want a look into the new China, if you plan to pop into the wholesale markets, if you are coming for the Trade Fair, after you get over the culture shock, you'll have a ball.

Getting There

BY TRAIN

From Hong Kong: KCR from Hung Hom. It's a 2-hour journey. You will use the East Railway Station in Guangzhou.

BY FERRY

From Hong Kong, there are four trips daily between Kowloon and Guangzhou, with departures from Hong Kong beginning at 7:30am and ending at 7:45pm. For the schedule from Guangzhou, call ✆ 8620/8222-2555.

BY AIR

Guangzhou has a new airport, Baiyun International, that is meant to rival Hong Kong's. It has been created to handle some 80 million passengers a year in the upcoming years and will be the area's largest air hub. There are now nonstop flights from Paris on Air France, flights from the U.S. (often through Tokyo) on a variety of carriers (including Northwest), and a host of Chinese flights. Although you probably won't fly from Hong Kong, service is available.

BY BUS

There was no train or ferry service from Macau to Guangzhou as we went to press. I took the bus, which was easy. You go to the Barrier Gate, cross into China, then cross the street and go down the escalator to the bus station. Buses leave every 15 minutes and cost about $5 one-way. The trip takes 2 hours unless traffic is bad. It's modern highway all the way. If your bus looks full or smoky, consider waiting for the next one. There is a bathroom stop after 1 hour, but no toilet on the bus.

Getting Around

Taxis are inexpensive; the flag falls at 7¥ (less than $1). I took taxis to far-flung areas that were over and under many freeways

Canton (Guangzhou)

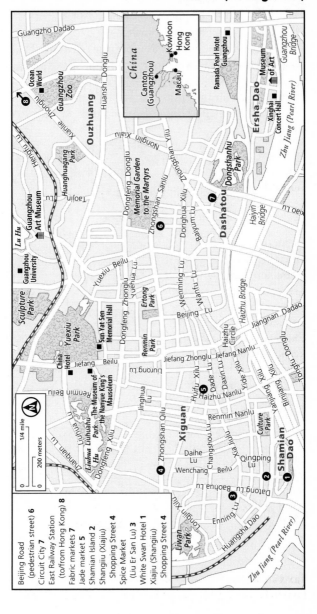

and way past where Grandma lives. The most I ever paid for a taxi was $5; you can go crosstown for $3.

If you take the bus from Macau, get off at the China Hotel (Marriott) and take a taxi to your chosen hotel. Taxis are easy to hail in the streets or at hotels.

Private pick-up and drop-off or shuttle transfers from the airport or train station can usually be arranged with your hotel.

There are two subway lines; both are relatively easy to use. But taxis are so cheap, why bother?

Calling Around

Guangzhou is in China, so you need the country code, 86, to call here. The area code for Canton is 020. If you have a new-fangled Chinese portable phone, it will automatically switch between Hong Kong and China zones. Otherwise, you will need to change SIM cards. SIM cards are sold on the trains.

The Lay of the Land

Guangzhou is a huge city, getting bigger as I type. For some reason, it reminded me of Caracas. I found it far more frightening than Beijing. Don't begin to think you can get a grasp on it in a day or two. Or in your lifetime. But then, you came to shop, and you won't be disappointed. Perhaps you should aim to just grasp your wallet and a few basics.

You can buy a book in Hong Kong called *Markets of Quangzhou* (available at Dymocks bookstores for $10) that has the addresses of all the wholesale buildings, but you can't possibly get to even a fraction of them. Time, energy, and ability to cope with a foreign environment will limit your explorations to just a few areas.

Note: Families who adopt babies seem to be plugged into a network of others who have already done so; they travel with their own shopping notes. Since adoption seems to mean 10 days in Guangzhou, there's a lot more time for exploration.

A Warning

Even old China hands are warned not to go into Canton's fresh food markets. The stories I have heard still haunt me. Also, don't look too carefully at those cages in front of restaurants. Just high-tail it (excuse the expression) out of there.

And while we're at it, in these days of epidemic and pandemic, stay away from bird markets.

Shopping Neighborhoods

You can get to Bar Street on your own. My list of shopping neighborhoods that are near the main hotels and easy to get to is below. And yes, I did travel into the Arab Quarter, and yes, I did track down various porcelain factories, and no, they are not listed below because I wasn't impressed.

Shamian Island: I haven't really figured out where the land ends and the island begins, but there's water all around once you get close to the White Swan Hotel. Behind the hotel is a strip of residential peace and quiet and greenery with sufficient tourist traps to keep you happy for a few hours. It's clean, safe, easy, and charming. There are several Starbucks-wannabe coffee joints as well as cutie-pie restaurants. Don't ask me why many of the shops offer to do laundry.

A TT (tourist trap) shop that I like a lot is **E-Gallery,** 61 Shamian Main St., which has a smaller branch around the corner closer to the White Swan in the strip of TTs there.

Shangiiu Shopping Street: Note that this Cantonese name is Xiajiu in Mandarin; same street, different dialect. This is one of the "new China" phenom streets and is especially fun in the evenings after people get off work. It's a pedestrian street where the locals go out for their promenade; many of the stores are malls and malls of tiny booths. My favorite building is **Liwan Plaza,** a mall with shops selling a jumble of fakes, new designers, and beauty services. There is a large (and somewhat legal) DVD shop in the front, facing the street. Legal DVDs cost 15¥ to 39¥ ($2–$6) and have holograms on them to signify they are legal, unless those are fake, too. Beauty treatments are good and cheap: I had a manicure ($8), hand-buffing treatment ($8), hand-hydrating and -whitening treatment ($10), and pedicure ($10).

Beijing Road: This is a different pedestrian street, not that different in feel from the Shangjiu/Xiajiu Shopping Street mentioned above, although farther from the White Swan Hotel. Here you'll find a famous local department store called Good Buy. I wasn't impressed by it because it is attempting to be a Western department store, but what do I know?

Jade Market: Adjoins some streets selling antiques in a warren of fun and alleys and stuff and possible good buys. Prices are seriously lower than in Hong Kong. From the street, there is merely a modern arcade of shops selling jade, beads, and semiprecious stones. Head inward to discover an entire village of lanes, with antiques shops to the rear. There is construction nearby, so check the location before you head out. For do-it-yourselfers, this alone is worth the trip just to load up on beads and gewgaws.

Spice Market (Liu Er San Lu): There are no dead or live birds, snakes, or dogs in this market. It's just heaps of gorgeous spices and beautiful textures and colors, all within walking distance of the White Swan Hotel. This is not for those who can't walk up and down many stairs because you will take a walkway over a freeway. Don't fret—street vendors sell illegal DVDs on the walkway.

Circuit City: There is an entire street of buildings called the Haiyin Electronics District. It is 1 block from the fabric markets, so you can do the whole thing in one swoop. The fabric markets feature home and fashion fabrics, although I was not particularly knocked out. The fabric market in Shanghai is far superior.

The electronics stores, however, are downright amazing. I spent hours here and feasted at McDonald's, which is conveniently located in the main shopping mall. Most of the DVD stores have video CDs on display. In most cases, you have to ask for English DVDs, then follow someone into a corridor. In some cases, the DVDs were right out in the open. The asking price was fairly good: about 7¥ (about $1) in most booths. (The *gweilo* price, for non-Asians, is 10¥/$1.20.)

Sleeping in Canton

WHITE SWAN HOTEL
Shamian Island

This hotel is so famous that it doesn't have a real street address. Indeed, it's at the end of a street, on a dead end against the point where two rivers merge, so it affords incredible water views. This is a member of Leading Hotels of the World. It's a modern building with a shopping mall, many restaurants, and what locals consider the best dim sum in southern China, home of dim sum.

The concierge team is great; they made all my train bookings for me and arranged the free shuttle to the train station when I was ready to return to Hong Kong. They hand out maps of the island as well as the city and have an extensive taxi card that lists the prime sites in town.

There is a Bank of China out the back door of the hotel, with an ATM. The neighborhood behind the hotel is filled with tourist shops; they all sell pink baby clothes because of the high percentage of girls adopted here.

Aside from the immediate tourist shopping district behind the hotel, there is a nearby spice market (no dogs), and you are walking distance (or a $2 taxi ride) from one of the main pedestrian shopping districts. There is shuttle bus service to the airport and the two train stations. For travel to Hong Kong, you want East Station.

Rates vary with room, view, and season; they begin at around $200 per night. Reservations through Leading Hotels of the World (© **800/223-6800** in the U.S.); local © 020/8188-6968. www.whiteswanhotel.com.

GARDEN HOTEL
368 Huanshi Dong Lu

This is the other top hotel in town; I have not stayed here. It's also modern. As the name suggests, it is built around a garden. Rates are similar to the White Swan Hotel's, about $200 a night for a double room. Local phone ✆ **8620/8333-8989.** www.gardenhotel-guangzhou.com.

WELCOME TO MACAU

The new Macau is even newer than the new Hong Kong, and the old, good, funky stuff has mostly been destroyed—except for the street where they make the antiques. The Chinese took possession in 1999, and the Las Vegas casinos arrived in 2004. Real estate is booming and architecture is looming, yet a resort feel prevails. Macau remains a luxury getaway destination where you can do a little shopping or gambling. The major furniture factories are on the Chinese side of Macau (Zhuhai) and are easy to shop as long as you have a visa.

Macau is a simple day trip from Hong Kong, or a weekend away. It has a new international airport, so you can also make it a main destination. This makes the most sense if you are going past the gates into the PRC and on to Guangzhou (Canton). On the other hand, shoppers who are shopping for pricey branded merchandise prefer Macau over Hong Kong because there is a $3 per $100 difference in the exchange rate. When you are spending $10,000 on an item, this adds up.

Why Macau?

As often as I go to Hong Kong, I rarely go to Macau—yet once I get to Macau, I kick myself for not having taken the time or trouble to visit. The colonial Portuguese architecture adjacent to modern high-rises gives you a glimpse of something very

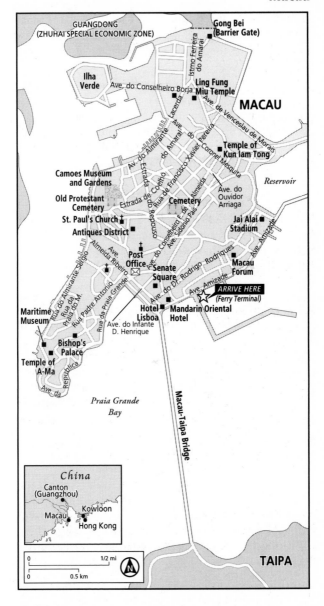

Macau

GUANGDONG
(ZHUHAI SPECIAL ECONOMIC ZONE)

Gong Bei
(Barrier Gate)

Ilha Verde

Ave. do Conselheiro Borja

Ling Fung Miu Temple

MACAU

Ave. de Venceslau de Morais

Istmo Ferreira do Amaral

Camoes Museum and Gardens

Av. do Almirante Lacerda

Estrada de Coelho

Ave. do Amaral

Rua de Francisco Xavier Pereira

Temple of Kun Iam Tong

Old Protestant Cemetery

Estrada do Repouso

Cemetery

Rua de Almeida

Ave. do Ouvidor Arriaga

Reservoir

St. Paul's Church

Antiques District

Ave. do Conselheiro F. de Almeida

Ave. Sidónio Pais

Jai Alai Stadium

Ave. Amizade

Post Office

Senate Square

Ave. do Dr. Rodrigo Rodrigues

Macau Forum

Ave. Ribeiro

Ave. Almeida

ARRIVE HERE
(Ferry Terminal)

Ave. Amizade

Mandarin Oriental Hotel

Hotel Lisboa

Ave. do Infante D. Henrique

Maritime Museum

Rua do Almirante Sérgio

Rua da Praia do M.

Rua Padre António

Rua da Praia Grande

Bishop's Palace

Temple of A-Ma

Ave. da República

Praia Grande Bay

Macau–Taipa Bridge

China

Canton (Guangzhou)

Macau

Kowloon

Hong Kong

TAIPA

| 0 | 1/2 mi |
| 0 | 0.5 km |

N

different from what you see in Hong Kong. The names on the shops and the Portuguese place names make the destination seem exotic. The atmosphere is laid back; the casinos offer a little bit of Las Vegas.

Macau's shopping is not great, but it is less expensive than Hong Kong's. If you are looking for furniture, waste no time in getting here. If you are interested in food, many come for the Portuguese-inspired home cooking. If you are in Hong Kong for only 3 days, don't burden your schedule, but if you have time, this trip expands your visual horizons.

Phoning Macau

If you're in Hong Kong and want to telephone or fax Macau for restaurant reservations, or whatever, the area code is 853. (The area code for Hong Kong is 852.)

The Lay of the Land

A 64km (40-mile) sea lane connects Macau to Hong Kong; it feels a million miles away. Macau itself is not an island, but the tip of a peninsula attached to mainland China. You can walk to the gate. You cannot walk through the gate without a visa. On the other side is the economic free zone of Zhuhai.

The "downtown" shopping and gambling area is in the older part of town, or what is left of it. The main drag's official name is Avenida Almeida Ribiero, but it goes by its Chinese name: San Ma Lo. The really fun stuff to browse is up the hill toward St. Paul's cathedral, but the main drag has stores and banks and my new favorite, the Pawnshop Museum.

The area alongside the ferry terminal has become hot real estate. You pass two malls before you reach the nearby luxe Mandarin Oriental. If you arrive by ferry, you'll need a bus or taxi to get into town; you will also need a taxi to get to various destinations. Your hotel or casino may provide a free shuttle bus.

Getting There

Your choices are simple: one if by air and two if by sea. Assuming you're not flying into Macau's international airport or crossing the hills from China, you are most likely coming from Hong Kong (near Central) and through **Shun Tak Centre,** or from the Kowloon side, at **China Hongkong City.**

Shun Tak Centre is the name of the modern, two-tower ferry terminal in Hong Kong's Western District. The MTR stop is Sheung Wan, which is the end of the line. The building and terminals are several floors up in the never-ending lobby space; ride several escalators and read a lot of signs.

China Hongkong City is in Kowloon on Canton Road, almost part of the mall complexes Harbour City and Ocean Terminal.

Fares fluctuate; variables include the day of the week, the time of day (night costs more), and the class of service (first costs more). First-class service on a weekday is HK$130 ($17) each way for an adult; departure tax adds another HK$25 ($3.25) or so. Weekends and holidays are about 10% more expensive; evenings after 6pm are also more costly. SuperClass, which costs HK$232 ($30) on weekdays and HK$247 ($32) on weekends, includes a meal.

Getting There Quickly

You can take a helicopter to the Ferry Terminal; it's a 16-minute journey. The fare is about $200, but it varies. For information, call © **852/2108-4838** in Hong Kong or visit http://api.air-macau.com.mo/en.

Travel Tips

Weekend prices are higher. Crowds are denser.

Don't travel on Chinese holidays, if you can help it.

If you plan to cross the border and go into China, there are a variety of visas available. Your options may also be based on what kind of passport you hold. There seems to be some prejudice against U.K. passport holders; they pay the most and have extreme limits put on their travels.

You can get your visa in Hong Kong before you leave, or in Macau. You can apply for a visa at the Barrier Gate (Gong Bei). For travel details, visit www.macautourism.gov.mo.

Arriving in Macau

You'll walk along a little gangway, enter a building, follow a walkway, and go through security. You are now in Portuguese Macau, and Portuguese is an official language. I spoke Portuguese to our taxi driver, who thought I was nuts. Better luck to you and yours.

Once you're outside the terminal, you'll note that there are bus stops and many lanes for cars, taxis, and tourist buses. It's a little confusing, partly because so much is going on. Persevere—your shuttle bus is waiting for you. Mandarin Oriental guests can report to the hotel's service desk inside the terminal and will be escorted to the waiting shuttle.

Also note that you are next door to the New Yoahan Shopping Centre, which is actually a Western-style department store with a fairly good grocery store. It also has a food court and clean bathrooms. Perhaps leave time for this adventure as you depart.

Money Matters

Macau has its own currency, the pataca (symbol MP$). Storekeepers will accept Hong Kong dollars but will give change in local currency. The two currencies are more or less at parity; HK$1 = MP$1.

US$1 = MP$8
1€ = MP$10
£1 = MP$15

Getting Around

Taxi flag falls at MP$10 ($1.35). Although taxi drivers have a destination chart in three languages, I promise you will not find a driver who speaks Portuguese. Use the Chinese chart or carry one from your hotel.

Shopping Macau

The main reason people come to Macau to shop is simple: The prices are lower than in Hong Kong, and the specialty is antiques and "antiques." Yes, they make 'em right here. These copies are so good that you will never buy another antique again, for fear that it just came out of the back room of a shop in Macau.

Every local from Hong Kong has his or her own private sources in Macau. Indeed, Macau is the kind of place where you need an inside track. There's no doubt that the really good stuff is hidden. And may be illegal.

The shopping must be considered fun shopping, unless you have brought along a curator from a museum or Sotheby's and really know your faux from your foo. If you give it the light touch, you're going to have a ball.

Sleeping in Macau

Metro Macau spreads over several islands, and most of the resort hotels are across a bridge. If you've come to shop, you probably want a central location and a luxury hotel. But understand that even in-town hotels specialize in a resort feel.

MANDARIN ORIENTAL
956 Av. da Amizade, Macau

For 20 years the most famous and fancy hotel in town, the Mandarin Oriental has a country-club atmosphere and amenities in a location between the ferry station and the heart of town.

There's big-name designer shopping and several great places to eat. My favorite is the Thai restaurant. Did I mention the spa? Rooms begin at $300, but there are deals, especially during the week. Note that, naturally, a harbor-view room costs more than one with a city view. U.S. reservations © 800/555-4288. Local © 853/567-888. www.mandarinoriental.com/macau.

Macau in a Day

Because addresses are hard to find in Macau, and many place names aren't clearly marked, the way for me to show you the best of central Macau's shopping area is to take you by the hand. If you are visiting Macau on a day trip, leave Hong Kong early so that you hit St. Paul's cathedral by 10am. Wander for a few hours and find lunch. Book the 4pm jetfoil back to Hong Kong.

- Tell your taxi driver *Igresia São Paolo* (St. Paul's Church), or be able to point to it on a map. A *Macau Mapa Turistica* is available free in Shun Tak Centre. This particular map has a picture of the church. St. Paul's was built in the early 1600s and burned to the ground in 1835, leaving only the facade, which is in more or less perfect condition. Not only is this quite a sight, but it's the leading tourist haunt in town and signals the beginning of the shopping and antiques district.
- The church is up a small hill, with two levels of stairs leading to a small square. If you go down both levels of the stairs, you will be at the major tourist-trap area and flea market heaven where dealers sell mostly new antiques . . . although you always hear stories of so-and-so, who just bought a valuable teapot at one of these stalls.
- Before you go lickety-split down all the stairs to the stalls, note that if you descend only one staircase, there is a small alley on the right side of the stairs—an alley that runs alongside the church. It's only a block long and ends just past the rear of the church, where you will find a tiny shrine.

- Not that it's well marked, but the name of this alley is **Rua da Ressureciao.** It's lined with tourist traps, porcelain shops, antiques stores, and even a ginseng parlor. Don't expect any bargains in these shops, and by all means know your stuff, but begin your shopping spree here. I must say that most of these stores are rather fetching: plates in the windows, red lanterns flapping in the breeze, maybe even a few carved dragons over the doorway. They all take credit cards, and you may have a ball.

- After you've done this alley, work your way around the vendors at the main "square" in front of the church steps. Film, soft drinks, and souvenirs are sold here; there are no particular bargains.

- Normal people now head into town by walking down the hill to the market and shopping as they go. The way to do this is to head down the Rua de São Paolo to the Rua da Palha, passing shops as you go. This walkway leads directly to the marketplace and the Senate Square, which is the heart of downtown. There are a few cute shops this way, and I have even bought from some of them.

- But I'm sending you down the hill the sneaky, nontouristy way. If you have the time, you may want to go down my way and then walk back up the main way so you can see the whole hill (and shop, of course). Also note that if you're with people and decide to split up, you can always meet back at the church stairway flea market area at an appointed time; this is a good place to get a taxi later on. Yes, I said flea market.

- The big red stall is not a toilet; it's a postal box. You can mail postcards here.

- If you are standing with the church to your back, a major tourist trap called **Nam Kwong Arts & Crafts** should be to your right, with the red postal box in front of it. (There are other branches of Nam Kwong in town.) Shop here if you are so inclined, then make a hard right (under the laundry from the balcony above) onto a small unmarked street.

Once you have turned right, look to the left for an alley called **Calcada do Amparo.** Enter here and begin to walk downhill.

- It's not going to be charming for a block or so, and you'll wonder where the hell you are and why all the tourists went in the other direction. Trust me, you're headed into the back alleys of the furniture and antiques area, as you will soon discover. You are wearing good walking shoes, I hope. This is the Tercena neighborhood, by the way.

- The reason I haven't given you shop names and addresses should now be abundantly clear—there's no way of really even knowing where you are when you walk down this hill. In about 2 blocks your alley will dead-end at a small street called **Rua Nossa Senhora do Amparo,** which may or may not be marked. These little alleys are called walkways or *travessas* and may have names (look for **Travessa do Fagao**).

- Get your bearings: You're now halfway to the main downtown square of Macau, on a small street that branches off from Rua do Mercadores, the main small shopping street that connects the main big shopping street to the area above at the top of the hill.

- This will make sense when you're standing there in the street, or if you look at a map. But don't look at a map too carefully because part of the fun of the whole experience is wandering around, getting lost and found, and feeling like what you have discovered is yours alone.

- When you are back on the Rua Nossa Senhora do Amparo, you'll find a ton of little dusty antiques shops. Some have names and some don't. They start opening around 11am; don't come too early. I wouldn't begin to vouch for the integrity of any of the shops here. I can only assure you that you'll have the time of your life.

- When you have finished shopping the antiques trade, work your way laterally across Rua das Estalagens to Rua do Mercadores. If you turn right, you will connect in a couple of short blocks to Avenida de Almeida Ribeiro, the main drag.

I suggest instead that you keep moving laterally so that you run smack into the market.

- The market is called **Mercado de São Domingos;** it has an outdoor fruit-and-veggie portion tucked into various alleys, an indoor livestock portion, and a dry-goods portion. Wander through as much as you can take, and find yourself at the main fountain and a square (Senate Sq.), which instinct will tell you is the main square. *Note:* There are still garment factories in Macau, and you will sometimes find name-brand merchandise in the market and side street near here.

- If instinct isn't enough, look for the restored colonial buildings, the tourist office, the main post office, the deliciously dilapidated Apollo Theatre, and the Leal Senado, which is the Senate building. You have arrived in the heart of town.

- The address of the tourist office (in case you need help, a place to meet up with the people you came with, or someone who speaks English and can teach you how to use the phone or write something for you in Chinese) is 9 Largo do Senado.

- The huge post office across the square is where you buy stamps, but beware: Lines can be long. Now you're on your own for lunch, more strolling, some gambling, or the return to the ferry.

- If you've chosen to spend a weekend night, surely you're up for the Night Market, which is similar to the Temple Street Market in Kowloon—complete with Chinese opera singers. Head to the **Cinema Alegria** to find the market, or ask your concierge to write it out for you in Chinese. The market is not far from the harbor and can be reached directly by bus. Taxis are cheap, so I went by taxi. Prices on junk and clothes without labels tend to be less than in Hong Kong; there are amazing amounts of baby clothes.

Gong Bei

Gong Bei is the Barrier Gate. I won't bore you with what it used to be like. Let's go with what it is now: fascinating but neither charming nor old-fashioned. This is big business, with millions of souls in transit. From the Macau side, your taxi will drop you at what looks like a modern office tower. Follow the crowds. In two steps, you exit Macau and then enter China. You must have a visa to enter China.

In this case, do not follow the crowds. Look for the immigration gates marked FOREIGN PASSPORTS. They are usually at the far right, if your back is to the front door.

Once you enter China, you wander through a lobby and outside, where a million watch salesmen will descend upon you. Ignore them and cross the street. To get to the bus station, take the escalators right in front of you down one level. Buy your ticket, and then go down another level into the bus station.

If you want a taxi for exploring the area (and going to furniture warehouses), head to the far side of the plaza *before* you go down the escalators.

About Zhuhai

Okay, so I'm running from A to Z in one sentence—who could resist? Just so you know, Zhuhai is the city across the Barrier Gate from Macau. It is one of those newfangled, fancy economic zones that are progressive and exciting for the Chinese while possibly unknown to the average tourist. This one has a fancy airport and Formula 1 racetrack, neither of which are much written about.

I like the idea of living here—I saw some gorgeous high-rise luxury apartment buildings with sea views. But I digress. The reason most people come here to shop is the furniture warehouses. And yes, the warehouses will arrange international shipping.

If you are interested in only the furniture part (that is, Zhuhai) and don't really care abut Macau or the Barrier Gate, you can take a ferry directly from Hong Kong to Zhuhai and back. Rush hour ends at 5pm, and there are not too many ferries back to Hong Kong after that, so watch the hour or have a backup plan.

The furniture warehouses spread across their own district; you will need a taxi that waits for you. Make sure you have all the information written in Chinese (easily obtained at your hotel concierge desk in Hong Kong). Bring cash to pay in Hong Kong dollars.

A bridge between Hong Kong and Zhuhai is scheduled to open in 2009.

Chapter Seven

....

HANOI

WELCOME TO HANOI
....

Some 60% of the Americans visiting Hanoi get there through Hong Kong, so here is your guide to one of the most fun shopping destinations you will ever encounter. Although I had some emotional reservations at first, once I got going and stopped crying, I was able to overcome. Bring U.S. dollars.

Getting There

The flight from Hong Kong is about 2 hours. Although there are various code shares, all flights are operated by Vietnam Airlines.

Hanoi is 1 hour behind Hong Kong.

Booking Hanoi

Air tickets bought in Hong Kong to Hanoi cost around $750, so I bought my tickets in Paris (where I live) for $450. (See p. 22 for information about my French travel agent.) My friends Peter and Louisa went with me—on the exact same flights—but bought a late-summer promotional package that included airfare, transfers, and 2 nights' hotel (as well as other perks) at the Sofitel Metropole for $650 each. Obviously, it pays to shop around.

Americans traditionally travel to Asia on a transpacific route, but you may want to investigate transatlantic fares. If you buy a low-cost coach fare to Paris, recover from jet lag, and then go on to Vietnam, you may save. I bought a promotional business-class ticket from Paris to Hong Kong on Cathay Pacific for $2,200 and booked the Vietnam leg separately.

Promotions & Packages

Because many people are still shaky about visiting Vietnam, there are a lot of packages that make it easy for you. The French have already discovered Hanoi as a vacation spot, so French tour operators have some fabulous deals. See above.

Sofitel has seasonal promotions called Getaway Invitations. For information in the U.S., call © **800/SOFITEL** or see www.sofitel.com. Note that there are two Sofitel hotels in Hanoi; the one you want is the Metropole.

Seasonally Yours

Prices and packages are related to the seasons, as in most destinations. Summers are hot and humid; you can get bargain prices in August. Fall and early winter are high season—Hanoi does a big Christmas and New Year's business. By January things slow down for Tet, the lunar new year, and then the rains start.

Arriving in Hanoi

You need a visa to enter Vietnam.

The Noi Bai International Airport is brand-new, modern, and gorgeous; entry is as easy as chopsticks.

Your hotel can arrange a pickup for you; package tours probably include transfers. You can easily take a taxi into town. Travel time is about 45 minutes. Emotional breakdown is optional.

Financial Matters

The official currency is the dong, which trades at about 14,500 to $1. However, U.S. dollars are accepted almost every place and are often preferred. Few stores accept credit cards. I didn't see any ATMs.

Yes, you can bargain in most stores. When the price is $2, it's hard to ask for a discount . . . but you can try.

The Lay of the Land

The main "downtown" shopping area is called the "District of the 36 Guilds" and consists of small streets and alleys that make up a village of shopping ops. This area is just north of Lake Hoan Kiem, locally referred to simply as "the lake."

The opera is southeast of the lake, and most of the luxury hotels are in the area between the opera and the southern shore of the lake. You can walk to the shopping district or take a taxi for very little money. Note that the Hotel Nikko Hanoi is not in this area but is closer to the southwestern section of the lake.

Getting Around

The luxury hotels (except the Nikko) are within walking distance of the best shopping parts of Hanoi.

Taxis are plentiful and inexpensive—a ride anywhere in the central shopping area costs $1. Pedicabs are cute but more expensive than taxis (and not air-conditioned)—expect to pay about $3 from your hotel to the shopping district.

Most luxury hotels have their own car service for transfers, day trips, and hourly rental. A car and driver costs about $30 an hour.

Renting a Car

You're kidding, right?

Sleeping Around

The country code for Vietnam is 84, and the city code for Hanoi is 4.

HANOI OPERA HILTON
1 Le Thanh Tong St.

This relatively new hotel (wisely, the name has been changed from the Hanoi Hilton) stands next door to the opera house, at the edge of the shopping district. It offers gold packages as well as the usual Hilton breaks and promotions. Rooms go for around $200. U.S. reservations © **800/HILTONS**. Local phone © **844/933-0500**. www.hilton.com.

HOTEL NIKKO HANOI
84 Tran Nhan Tong St.

This location is a little off-center for me, although the hotel has very nice shops, and taxis are cheap. The area is Hai Ba Trung, often called the HBT district—"how 'bout that" is all I can call it. It's near the "other" lake (Thien Quang). U.S. and Canada reservations © **800/NIKKO-US**. Local phone 844/822-3535. www.nikkohotels.com.

SOFITEL METROPOLE HANOI
15 Ngo Guyen St.

The Sofitel Metropole prides itself on being shopping head-quarters; it offers a Born to Shop package and provides all guests with a locally written (and updated) map and shopping resource list. This is the historic hotel in town—the *grande dame* in a super location. Promotional rates sometimes list two prices, for the modern wing of the hotel and the older portion. The modern wing costs less.

Expect to pay about $150 for the new part and $250 or more for the old part if you get a promotional rate. Don't miss a meal in the Spices restaurant, whether you stay here or not.

Hanoi

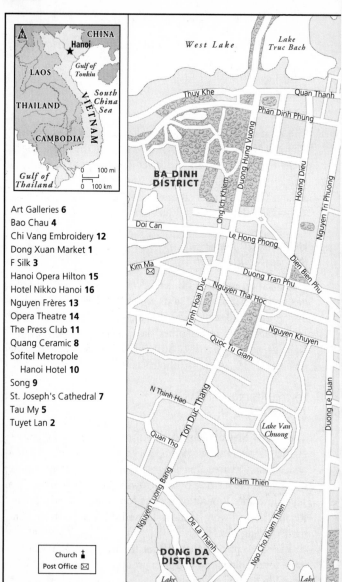

Art Galleries **6**
Bao Chau **4**
Chi Vang Embroidery **12**
Dong Xuan Market **1**
F Silk **3**
Hanoi Opera Hilton **15**
Hotel Nikko Hanoi **16**
Nguyen Frères **13**
Opera Theatre **14**
The Press Club **11**
Quang Ceramic **8**
Sofitel Metropole
   Hanoi Hotel **10**
Song **9**
St. Joseph's Cathedral **7**
Tau My **5**
Tuyet Lan **2**

Church ⚰
Post Office ⊠

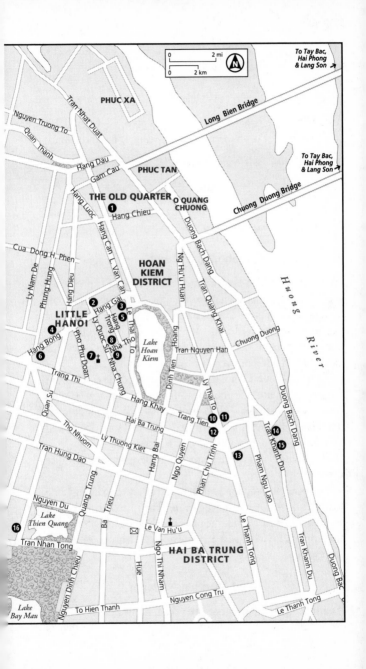

U.S. reservations ✆ 800/SOFITEL. Local ✆ 844/826-6919. www.accorhotels.asia.com.

Watch It!

Although there is a business in war souvenirs, I could not stomach the idea of shopping for them. Rumor has it that most are fakes.

Watch It! 2

Stores come and go so rapidly that it's impossible for any guidebook to be totally accurate.

Shopping Hanoi

I spent a weekend in Hanoi amid various reports from friends and colleagues about where to find the best shopping. Some thought that because Hanoi has always been in communist hands, it would have less of an understanding of retail. They suggested Saigon, now named Ho Chi Minh City (written locally as HCMC) or even Hoi-An.

As it turns out, Hanoi has quickly grasped the concepts of the glam slam and the good deal. It has stores that would do Paris, New York, or Tokyo proud. The locally made merchandise is far more sophisticated than in Hong Kong and China; designer and brand business is just getting going. Obviously, you don't go to Vietnam to buy designer merchandise anyway.

I shopped nonstop for 3 full days and returned to Hong Kong kicking myself for not buying more. The raw authenticity of the setting is pure charm; the prices are heaven (few items cost more than $25; most cost $3) and you can truly shop 'til you drop.

Good Morning, Vietnam

Pronouncing anything properly was a talent that eluded me throughout my visit. I did note that Hanoi is often written as

Ha Noi, which may be confusing at first. Travel with addresses written down and a card from your hotel so you can always get back there.

Note that when written out, many street names are so similar that you can get confused—Hang Bong and Hang Trong are two different streets.

I was also surprised at how few people on the streets speak French.

Shopping Days & Hours

Stores are open seven days a week. Some close for lunch. Hours are normally 9am to 6pm. Stores close during Tet, the new year celebration, sometime in January or early February.

Markets

1912 Market: This market is named for a date in December, so you say *nineteen twelve*. It sells everything.
Dong Xuan: A series of street markets and market buildings not too far from the cathedral, a tad rough but very low cost.

Street Vendors

Street vendors abound. Most sell the same old stuff: postcards and guidebooks, along with a few Graham Greene titles (*The Quiet American* is the most popular). The books appear to be photocopies of page proofs or computer printouts. Be warned that these books are pretty hard on the eyes and have numerous typos.

International Brands

Brands are just discovering Vietnam and vice versa. Hanoi currently has a short string of brand-name stores ranging from **Pierre Cardin** (which looks nothing like anything you might guess was French) to **l'Occitane,** which is identical to its stores all over the world. The Sofitel Metropole has a very spiffy branch of **Louis Vuitton.** There are no bargains.

Western Merchandise

Most of the hotels have gift shops that sell American and European magazines. The **Press Club**, 59A Ly Thai To, behind the Metropole, sells cookbooks in English and in French. The Metropole has a grocery store that sells French foodstuffs.

Hanoi Overkill

Excuse the expression, but please note that after a few hours of shopping, you may get a headache, have crossed eyes, or fall into that unfortunate state in which everything looks alike and you want to run away screaming. There is so much merchandise, and it is so gorgeous and so inexpensive, that you can lose your mind. Apocalypse at any moment. Let the shopper beware.

Best Buys

Ceramics: If you want the dish on dishes, I'm the wrong person to talk to because I went nuts buying ceramics—vases, place settings, everything. I even took an excursion to a village that sells only ceramics (p. 192). The problem is that shipping brings up the cost and packing adds to weight and worries. Still, I had no breakage, and I only regret that I had to give up two vases in Hong Kong when I couldn't carry them on the plane.

Ceramics from northern Vietnam are superior to others because of the qualities of the local clay. Various villages specialize in different styles; you can also buy at the market in beautiful downtown Hanoi.

Chopsticks: I am not talking "with six you get egg roll" chopsticks—I am talking about an art form. Fancier stores sell chopsticks by the set ($2–$5 per set), but you can buy them in sets for 10 people for $6 at the market. They do not go in the dishwasher.

Contemporary art: I rarely report on art because taste in art is so personal. I was shocked and amazed by the number of art galleries, however, and the quality of the wares and diversity of styles. Most of the contemporary art does depict local subjects, but I bought a small oil painting of a house that could be in Vietnam or the south of France. Many of the artists are highly collectible; many have regular shows in Hong Kong and Europe.

Embroidery: One of the smaller stores I liked was **Tuyet Lan,** 182 Hang Bong St.

Ethnic Fashion: The good thing about these items is that they are fashionably ethnic and funky without being costumey or native-dress Halloweeny. You can buy the traditional dress style, called an *ao dais*—what I call a Madame Nu dress, but that dates me. There are crinkle skirts and wraparound trousers, embroidered shoes, and all sorts of items that could turn up on the pages of *Vogue.*

Foodstuffs: I fell in love with a small shop named **Hoa Qua Kinh Do,** 33 Hang Buom, which sells only locally made fruit products. There were eight kinds of apricot jam alone. Foodies shouldn't miss it.

Horn: It's not tortoise shell, it's buffalo horn.

Lacquer: Forget touristy concepts and Disney styles—this is the most sophisticated, drop-dead-chic lacquer you have ever seen. Major home-style stores in Europe and the U.S. are already overcharging for it.

Lanterns: Assorted lantern styles are available, but the most popular—and chic—is the style called Indochine, a sort of tulip-bulb shape in various sizes made of silk and usually finished off with a tassel. Prices begin at around $7.

Shoes: Believe it or not, shoes must be made here because there are tons of them. I actually even found a size 41 (American size 10)! I bought some embroidery raffia mules on a princess heel for $36 at the Sofitel Metropole hotel. If your feet are a more common size, try the shoe market at Pho Hang Dau.

Silk: Aside from the usual, you'll see silk duvet covers and hand-stitched silk quilts. **Song,** 5 and 7 Nha Tho, has the fanciest merchandise in town, but there are several classy shops and many others that sell the chic stuff. **F Silk,** 82 Hang Gai St., is worth a look, if only because it is a Fendi look-alike in decor and logo. I bought several shirts in silk and in linen at **Ngoc Hien,** 58 Hang Gai St. I liked the style so much that I then had the shirt made in English cotton (complete with monogram on the cuff) in Hong Kong.

Tailoring: Many report that custom tailoring is a breeze. I didn't have the time or budget.

Great Gifts

Just about everything in the city costs less than $5, but scoring great gifts for under $3 is still a good game to play. I also found a large variety of $10 gifts that looked like they cost $50.

Hotel Shopping in Hanoi

All of the luxury hotels have some shopping. Prices in hotels are much higher than on the street, but the merchandise may be chosen or displayed so that it's easier to enjoy. The Sofitel Metropole has the only Louis Vuitton shop in town and will be adding some French names, and its gift shop has several good buys—including a wooden salt-and-pepper box for $10 that is so chic I gave one to superchef Alain Ducasse.

The Nikko has a French bakery (!) and a fabulous store for fashion and embroidery. The upstairs crafts shop is nothing special.

Best Shopping District in Hanoi

Thirty-six Pho Puong is the District of the 36 Guilds, the old quarter where each trade had its own little alley. The word *hang* tells the shopper that this is indeed a street of merchandise, and the word that comes next says what kind of merchandise. Hang Gai is one of the leading streets for silks and embroideries. It's in the center of town near the cathedral.

Hanoi's Best Shopping Street

You'll find the best stores, but not necessarily the best prices, on **Nha Tho,** a short street in the heart of the shopping district, on the side of Nha Chung, a more mainstream shopping street. Nha Chung means Church Street; the street runs alongside St. Joseph's Cathedral. The good stores include **Song** (see below), **Mosaique, Kien Boutique,** and LaCasa.

The Best Stores in Hanoi

Bao Chau
48 Hang Bong St.

In including this on my best-of list, I am advising that part of what is so wonderful about this store is its location on a street filled with great stores laden with lacquerware. This store is unusual in that it has a mix—real and fake antiques, crafts, gift items, and so on. I saw many items here that I did not see elsewhere. The store also had the best price on raffia embroidered handbags, which elsewhere are about $30 and here were $16.

Chi Vang Embroidery
17 Trang Tien

This large store is on an up-and-coming retail street that is close to the Hilton and the Metropole, but slightly out of the mainstream downtown shopping district. It's worth the walk for the architecture of the building and the merchandise—more chic embroidery than you can imagine, at prices that will make your palms sweat. I saw an entire bed set for $150. Don't forget to go upstairs.

CoCoon
30 Nha Chung

I went downright nuts in this store—everything whispered my name, from the shawls to the bathrobes. I bought handbags, tote bags, drawstring silk pouches, and then more bathrobes. I bought so much that I got a 15% discount. I tried to charge it, but the sales clerk was not adept at using Visa and kept saying my card had expired.

L'Image
34 Nha Chung

The store specializes in tabletop crafts made from wood, silver, horn, lacquer, ceramics, and fabrics. Very chic.

Nguyen Frères
3 Phan Chu Trinh St.

This is not in the regular downtown shopping area but is within walking distance of the Metropole. It is a house turned into a store that sells home decor—sort of the glam Indochine look. Remember that lamps are 220 volt and must be converted for the U.S.; furniture has to be shipped. But thankfully, there are some small items for table accessorizing and gift giving.

Nia-Nia
63 Hang Bong

This is an art gallery that also sells lacquer, a somewhat strange mix of product. Nonetheless, the selection impressed me, and, yes, I did buy a painting here. In fact, I considered buying everything here.

Quang Ceramic
63 Hang Trong

This is not a cutie-pie shop and may not really even be a consumer shop—it sort of feels like a hotel supply showroom. Not all of the ceramics are attractive (to my taste), but some of the wares are both stunning and inexpensive. A teapot with six cups was sold as a set only, for $12. I bought many things that I swear were twins of items I saw at Armani Casa in Milan. The company takes credit cards and even shows in Germany. www.quangceramic.com.

SONG
5 and 7 Nha Tho

Be still my heart. This is one of the best stores in the world. I can't quite tell you how powerful it is, partly because it is so shocking to find a store this unique and this chic in the middle of Hanoi. The brainchild of an Australian designer, Song sells home style in one shop and women's fashion in the other. Note that prices are high for local surroundings, and you can find some of the same merchandise around town for less. Prices are low compared to Barneys, though.

TAU MY
16 Hang Trong

There is no question that this is one of the best embroidery stores in town; it is also expensive. Of course, expensive by local standards is not necessarily expensive in the real world.

Tours

TOUR #1: ONE PERFECT DAY IN HANOI

- Begin with a good breakfast—despite the French influence and the notion of continental breakfast, you may want to hit a breakfast buffet and load up on carbs. Don't forget to drink lots of liquids, especially if it's hot and humid. And as you leave on this tour, grab a bottle of water for your tote bag. Yes, you will have to make bathroom stops, but your body needs water in this climate and you don't want to poop out before the tour is over.
- Now might be a good time to try a pedicab—they are more expensive than taxis, but fun. Your destination is "the Cathedral"—technically, Saint Joseph's, but locally referred to as just "the Cathedral." Make sure you have agreed on the price of the pedicab before you set off on the journey— you could be cheated otherwise. If the fee is more than $3, something is wrong . . . or you have pedaled in from the airport.

- The Cathedral is on a little square that abuts **Church Street** (Nha Chung)—this is an excellent shopping thoroughfare and a good place to start the day. Use the Cathedral as your home base and "know your way around" point. It's also always easy to get a taxi or a pedicab here.

- Work both sides of the street rather than up and down—this will save time, and you will not be returning this way on this tour—although you can make a detour if you need to buy more. Do it all in one visit, if you can, at least getting your bearings, learning the merchandise and the prices. The street looks a tad funky, but there are many fancy stores here. There is good shopping up 1 block and then to your left (west) from the Cathedral, so don't miss anything.

- Walk west (away from the Sofitel) on Nha Chung for 1 shopping block and then turn right on **Nha Tho** Street. This street is only 1 block long but has fabulous stores, including two different shops named **Song** (see above)—an Australian creation that is simply one of the best stores in the world. Drool or buy.

- You should work Nha Tho Street up one side and down the other. But don't forget the turnaround spot at Hang Trong. You might not see the street sign, but never mind—you will see two or three stalls dead ahead of you that sell silk lanterns and lacquerware. Don't hesitate to buy.

- So now you are headed south on Nha Tho, essentially on the other side of the street from Song, where there are more great stores, such as **Caprice** and **Mosaique.** This short meander onto Nha Tho will bring you back to the main Church Street and you will turn right, with Song to your rear. Do note that Nha Chung (Church St.) has become Ly Quoc Su . . . this will confuse you when you look at addresses or business cards, but essentially this is still the same main thoroughfare that is home base.

- Continue shopping another block, and then turn left onto **Hang Gai,** which is the art gallery street.

- Follow Hang Gai until you come to a crooked crossroads—you can actually take any of these streets and get lost and found as you shop them all. For tour purposes, choose Hang Bong and continue to shop.

- When you reach the main street, Pho Trang Thi, you can take a taxi back to your hotel, or to the Sofitel Metropole for a cold drink.

TOUR #2: BACK-STREET HANOI

- This tour begins at the Sofitel Metropole, where you will want to look at the gift shops. You may not need the Louis Vuitton shop (it's the real thing), but there are a few shops that sell some great stuff. This is a chance to poke around the hotel property if you are not staying here.
- Walk out of the old building of the hotel, past the pool and into the new part of the hotel, and then right out onto the back street, Ly Thai To. You'll see several shops as you go to your right (if the hotel is to your rear)—you are shopping your way to the **Opera House,** just a block or 2 away. You might also want to look at the cafes and restaurants in this block—we enjoyed several of them.
- The Opera House stands at a crossroads. Here you turn right onto Trang Tien and shop your way south (toward the Cathedral). This is an up-and-coming shopping street, not totally developed as we go to press, but this is Back-Street Hanoi, and the whole thing is worth it just to stop at a shop named **Broderie,** 36 Trang Tien.
- When you get back to Pho Hang Bai, essentially the front of the Sofitel (you have walked around a big block), take a taxi to the Dong Xian market. This is more of a market area, slightly off-center from the heart of town. The market is more of a neighborhood of buildings and alleys and street action, so work it to your heart's content.
- Take a taxi directly to **Quang Ceramic,** 63 Hang Trong, but only if you are interested in dishes, dishes, dishes.
- An alternate: If you don't want to make the stop for ceramics, take a taxi to the **1912 Market,** in the Hai Ba Trung district. This is an enormous covered market, very real and not for the timid.

- Another alternate: Should your idea of a dish be edible and should you not want to visit the ceramics, instead take a taxi to **Hoa Qua Kinh Do,** 33 Bang Boum. The tiny shop sells fresh fruits, confits, and jams—all local and quite unusual. Then you can opt for the 1912 Market, described above.

- When you are done with the markets, take a taxi to **Nguyen Frères,** 3 Phan Chu Trinh, one of the fanciest interior-design shops in town, a few blocks behind the Sofitel Metropole.

- Now you are just a few blocks from the Opera House and more or less where you started. You can call it quits or walk around the streets that encircle the Metropole—there's even a **street of booksellers,** where the fronts of the stores are still marked in Cyrillic.

- If you're game, continue walking toward the Cathedral on the book street or one street over—Pho Trang Thi—for another block until you get to a modern, Art Deco–style building across the street from Vietnam Airlines. This is a modern Western-style mall with rather boring shops, except for the supermarket. Now's the time to load up on noodles and fish sauce.

Excursion to Bat Trang

Once I found out that there was an entire village of ceramics shops, I was off and panting. We hired a taxi for the half-day excursion and paid about $40. The drive took almost an hour. Naturally, the driver took us to the stores where he knew people; he was a tad sulky when I insisted on doing the whole town.

The town is larger than you think, and shopping it all takes a good eye and a strong back. In no time at all, everything starts to look alike. I have heard of people who hated it here, mostly because there is a lot of junk and they don't care if the vases cost $3. I had the time of my life, although I bought little and was exhausted afterward.

Departing Hanoi

Remember that you are most likely flying to another Asian or European city, so you go on the kilo system, not the piece system. Show an onward-bound ticket for leniency.

Departure tax is paid after you check your luggage. Note that because Chinese airports now charge their departure tax in a ticket, you may not be used to the concept of "departure tax" or the need to stand in a different line to pay it.

Chapter Eight

....

SHANGHAI

WELCOME TO SHANGHAI

....

As you read this, my apartment is for sale and I am applying for a doggy visa so that Samantha Joe Cocker Spaniel and I can move part-time to Shanghai. I keep telling her, "Toto, they're not Communists anymore." She keeps telling me her name isn't Toto.

Indeed, lovers dancing on rooftops overlooking the river, a veritable *bong*-uette at the Cupola, big-name French chefs popping up everywhere, and top Australian tastemaker David Laris doing spicy chocolates on the side when not cooking at one of the town's snazziest new restaurants. It was once the Paris of the East, the Whore of Asia . . . you should see the old girl now.

Shanghai is one of the most exciting cities in the world. Westerners are welcome; the new Shanghai seduces you with the delicious state of euphoria generated by luxury hotels, fine restaurants, clean streets, and fabulous shopping. All those antiques and DVDs can't possibly be fake, can they?

There's dinner for two at about $50 a head at a restaurant that would cost four times that in London or New York; there's the world's largest Louis Vuitton store; there's a brand-new circular train station (South Station) that required the invention of the world's first circular crane for construction to be

---

Electronically Yours: Shanghai

- Always check for hotel deals: www.asia-hotels.com.
- Shanghai Tourist Information & Service Center: www.tour info.sh.cn.
- Shanghai on the Internet: www.sh.com.
- Three on the Bund (lifestyle concept with restaurants, retail, and Evian spa): www.threeonthebund.com.
- Custom tailor W. W. Chan & Sons Ltd.: www.wwchan. com.

---

completed . . . it looks like a sports stadium ready for the World Series. Oh, and I forgot the most important metaphor of them all—the new Formula 1 race course. Gentlemen, start your engines. Next stop: Shanghai.

If you're expecting a honky-tonk scene or the sing-song girls pictured on cigarette cards and calendars—forget it, pal. This is the new world, with clear intentions of burying Hong Kong. Frankly, I don't think Honkers is ready to go down so fast—but then, I'm not Chinese, and I am going to apply for residency.

GETTING THERE

See chapter 2 for information about carriers and Asian travel details; the information here is more city specific.

Arrival by Air

Shanghai has two international airports; most international flights serve the newer one, Pudong. The other airport, Hong Qiao, was being renovated at press time. In the next few years, the two airports are expected to welcome some 80 million people a year—each.

You can fly nonstop to Shanghai on transpacific routes from the U.S., transcontinental routes from Europe, transpolar routing from the U.K., and from Down Under via Dubai or Australia. I frequently go to Shanghai from Hong Kong; there is a Dragonair flight just about every hour.

If you arrive in Shanghai from an international destination (including Hong Kong), you will be asked to fill in a landing card and will, of course, already have a visa. You may also have to fill in a health card. The lines move quickly; you will be through immigration in no time, waiting at carousels for your luggage. Luggage carts are available.

About that visa: Don't panic. Under some circumstances, you don't need a visa—if you are in the country less than 48 hours with a group (possibly on a cruise) or you hold a passport from 1 of the 17 countries that have recently relaxed their relationship with China and waived the visa requirement.

Americans and Brits do need visas. For more on how to obtain a visa as an American citizen, see p. 18.

The Pudong Airport is one of Shanghai's new architectural highlights, with lots of glass and light, reflecting the latest trend in airports that resemble museums. This airport is so well hidden in the middle of nowhere that you may be shocked at how far out it is. Don't worry about the distance, or about the fact that you may have to stand in line for 30 to 50 minutes if you want a legal taxi. You sure don't want an illegal one, so ignore those bozos who ask to ferry you about town.

After clearing formalities, you go to the hotel desk for your transfer—or outside for a taxi. Driving time from the Pudong International Airport to the Sofitel JJ Oriental in Pudong is about 45 minutes, so figure at least an hour to a hotel on the other side of the Bund or in Shanghai proper. Also remember to allow for traffic problems—it could take longer.

The big news is that there is a fast train—one of those fancy maglev jobs—from the Pudong Airport right to Pudong. The bad news: This train doesn't go directly to downtown Pudong. It stops at Long Yang Road; you can change there for a train to downtown Pudong or deeper into Shanghai.

The maglev train also serves Hong Qiao Airport, a stop on the green line, which was under construction as we went to press. Do not confuse the airport stop with the Hongqiao Road stop on the blue line.

Money on Arrival

If you have not arranged a hotel pickup, which will be charged to your room, you will need yuan for paying your taxi fare. If you don't have any on you, there's a nice long line and an exchange booth. The ATM is at the departure gate.

Arrival by Cruise Ship

Shanghai's importance to China has always been its port; today many cruise ships call here at a number of berths on the Huangpu River; the fancier ships usually get berths near the Bund.

Train Travel

You may want to travel within China by train—I regularly use the overnight service between Shanghai and Beijing. Whether you are coming or going, your biggest problem will be luggage. If you are arriving in Shanghai, don't plan to meet up with friends for a ride or help with those bags—there are four exits, and it can be very confusing. (I fear Peter and Louisa are still waiting for me.)

If you are departing Shanghai by train, there is no need to rush to the station "to be safe" because you will not be allowed out of the lounge area until 30 minutes before the train leaves. The lounge area is quite nice (for China), but you are a long way from done with the journey—you may have to go up an escalator, trek down a hall, climb down sets of stairs, and walk a mile along the platform before you find your car. Should your nerves be strung anything like mine, or your luggage pile be half the size of mine, you will find this a rather tense adventure . . . until you are onboard and marveling at how chic the train is (complete with video screens).

Porters are not plentiful and are normally banned from taking you directly to the platform or from actually loading the luggage onto the train for you. This can be overcome with an extra ticket—I usually buy all four of the beds in a compartment, even if there aren't four of us traveling. Those who can easily manage their luggage were not born to shop.

Various Metro lines serve the city's new South Station, which is considered a revolutionary architectural project. This station will probably change the face of travel in and out of Shanghai. Negotiations to connect Shanghai and Beijing by bullet train in time for the Olympics in 2008 are under way. This will reduce the travel time to 4 to 5 hours.

THE LAY OF THE LAND

If you're familiar with Hong Kong, you'll quickly understand my Hong Kong parallels. Pudong is the equivalent of Kowloon—the boomtown on the far side of the river. Today it has an impressive array of towers and tenants, all with breathtaking views of the waterfront promenade known as the Bund. In 10 years (maybe in 10 min.), Pudong could rival "downtown."

But wait—Pudong is far more than a contained space on the "other side of the river"—it is an enormous metro area and includes much, much more than what we have been led to believe is the sum total of the city. On my last visit, I accidentally booked myself into the Sofitel Pudong, thinking I was going to be next to the Hyatt, and discovered a whole new part of town that turned out to be very convenient for the airport and downtown. Consider this the "new territories" of Pudong. If you've never been to Hong Kong, don't fret. You can still find your way around simply by realizing that a river separates the two parts of town and that the giant Pearl Tower is in Pudong, on the far side of the river.

The city of Shanghai (Pu Xi) lies on the west bank of the Huangpu River. The neighborhoods bear the traces of the original Chinese city (though the walls are long gone) and the foreign concessions, or territories, of the 19th century (the French concession is still the nicest). Despite its size, there actually is a system, especially for the streets in "downtown": North-south streets are named after Chinese provinces, and east-west streets after Chinese cities. Of course, you need to learn your provinces in order to use this information—or keep a map on you at all times.

GETTING AROUND

Traffic is bad and will only get worse. I recently suffered a shopping adventure outside of town that took over an hour to reach—yet only 20 minutes on the return to my hotel. Even the leap from Pudong into "town" can take time if you get stuck in traffic.

Taxis

Taxis are inexpensive and, especially at hotels, plentiful. There are new, clean cars and fleets that can be identified by their livery colors, such as metallic soft green or Bordeaux lacquer. The good taxi companies give you a receipt (keep it) and promise that if you were cheated, you will get your money back, plus some. Drivers don't expect to be tipped. You can hail a taxi on the street, but if this method doesn't work for you, find one at any hotel. Among locals, some favor only taxis from specific firms. White gloves are optional but are indicative of a higher level of service.

I stumbled upon a taxi driver with a van I loved, had some Chinese friends make a deal with him, and used him as my private car and driver for $10 an hour.

Private Cars

Most luxury hotels do a good business in private cars; this pays if you have lots of stops to make or need to be dressed up for appointments. Fees are based on the type of car and length of

Shanghai Orientation

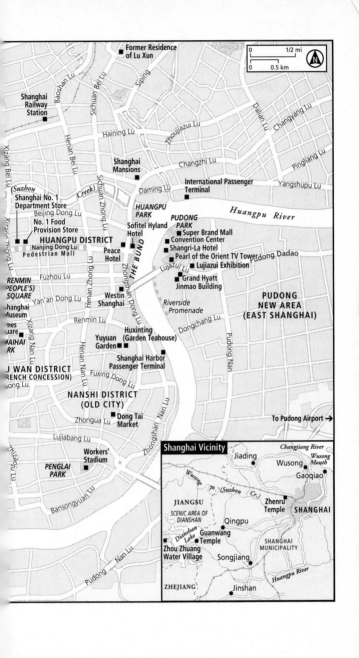

time; there are also flat fees for airport transfers and for day trips. Half a day in a Lexus costs about $125; a car to Suzhou for the day (and back) is about $300. A private taxi company can also provide a car and driver, but it is unlikely that the driver will speak English. Expect to pay about $60 for the day trip to Suzhou.

Metro

Shanghai has a great Metro system, but it's not very extensive (see map, p. 203) nor is it as clean as Beijing's. It's not a summer sport. If you ride during non–rush hours, you should be fine. Note that line No. 4 is under construction as we go to press; it is a circle line in the central part of Shanghai and is most useful.

The official names are Metro Line 1, Metro Line 2, and so forth. A different color designates each line. Note that all station names are written in pinyin and that the Renmin Guangchang station is also called People's Square.

Line 2 serves Pudong and connects the two international airports; in so doing, it connects the two sides of the city. Metro Line 3 is an east-west sort of transverse, all on the Shanghai side of the river and crossing the Suchow Creek.

Important Announcement

No matter where you go or how you get around town, make sure you have one of the hotel cards on you that says "My hotel is . . . ." Hotels give them out by the zillion. Most hotels also have short charts of addresses in English and Chinese and often also in pinyin so you can point to where you want to go and show it to the driver. Take it from me: No Chinese person will understand your pinyin pronunciation of anything more extravagant than hello: *nihau* ("knee-how").

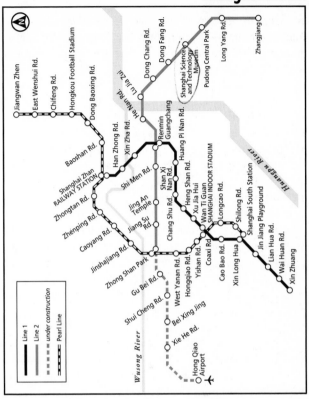

Shanghai Metro

About Addresses & Guidebooks

A guidebook to China is a good starting point, but no guidebook—especially a printed and bound one from a bookstore, library, or online bookseller—can keep up with the changes in China, especially in Shanghai. Buildings and stores are being torn down in Shanghai so fast that they can disappear overnight. Add to that the long lead time in rewriting and publishing books, and there's no telling how accurate any guide will be.

This problem doesn't exist just with guides; many (maybe most) concierges don't know what's going on, either. No one in Shanghai can keep up with the changes. Hearsay—even concierge hearsay—is cheap and cannot be trusted. Sometimes you just have to get out there and see for yourself.

SLEEPING IN SHANGHAI

The new Shanghai has attracted enough business travelers over the last decade to ensure that there are plenty of suitable hotels with Western-style amenities. Just about every big, four-star chain already has at least one hotel here, and it is not unusual for a chain to have a hotel on each side of the river.

Because Shanghai is so spread out, where you stay can be important to how you feel about the city; on the other hand, where you stay doesn't matter that much because little in Shanghai is within walking distance and taxis are cheap.

Do note that hotels always have promotional rates, depending on their occupancy rate or the phases of the moon. Ask. When the **Shangri-La** opened in Pudong, rates began at $138. **Ritz-Carlton** had a summer special for Visa cardholders of $130 per night on the weekend and $150 per night on weekdays. The **Peninsula** chain has broken ground on a property near the British Embassy, and the city's first luxury boutique hotel, **Bund 18,** has opened, yes, on the Bund.

Also remember that Westin, Sheraton, and St. Regis chains are all part of the Starwood group. The Westin had a winter rate of about $200, while the St. Regis—in a far corner of Pudong—was about $180. Location counts.

Be sure to ask about upgrades, and don't grab the least expensive room. Because the better hotels court business travelers, they all have executive floors with many perks that often make paying more a bargain.

Shanghai Central (Pu Xi)

HILTON SHANGHAI
250 Hua Shan Rd. (Metro: Jing An Temple or Chang Shu Rd.)

This was one of the first Western hotels in town and is somewhat famous for providing comforts. There's a mall, the W. W. Chan tailor shop from Hong Kong is here, and the hotel has several restaurants and old-fashioned newly restored Hilton style. The location is a little off-center, but taxis are cheap and rates are reasonable. Good concierge service; free shuttle buses. The fabu bar on the top floor of the hotel boasts lovely decor, comfy chairs, and a view of Shanghai. Also good: the Sichuan restaurant alongside the bar. *Note:* You have a choice of nearby Metro stations.

On a promotional deal, you can get this hotel at $129. During a recent Formula 1 event, rooms were $450. U.S. reservations ✆ 800/HILTONS. Local ✆ 021/6248-0000. www.hilton.com.

Okura Garden Hotel
58 Mao Ming Nan Lu (Metro: Shi Men Rd.)

In terms of shopping, this hotel has a super location—right in the heart of the part of town that was once the French concession. The building is the former French Club. In terms of luxury, this is the latest in Japanese chic. Commonly called the Garden Hotel, it opens onto a garden. You feel quite elegant, civilized, and contented to arrive here . . . and if it's winter, you will adore the heated toilet seats as well as other Japanese amenities and inventions geared toward spoiling you.

The hotel lobby has several stores; the Metro stops within walking distance. The hotel is a member of Leading Hotels of the World.

Rooms are about $350 per night. U.S. reservations ✆ 800/223-6800. Local ✆ 021/6415-1111; fax 021/6415-8866. www.gardenhotelshanghai.com.

Portman Ritz-Carlton
Shanghai Centre, 1376 Nanjing Xi Lu (Metro: Jing An Temple)

The fanciest and possibly best hotel in Shanghai, this is the standard by which all others must measure themselves. The executive floors offer lounge privileges that really make a difference in the comfort of your stay and more than balance out the price of the upgrade with the perks you gain. There is also an excellent business center and what many expats say is the best hairdresser in town.

The hotel is large, and I think the concierge staff downstairs is overworked, which is one reason it pays to upgrade to a room that has use of the lounge and its private concierge service—which is fabulous.

Regular rooms cost under $200 a night; it's usually about $50 more per night for the club rooms, which pay for themselves in extras. U.S. reservations © 800/241-3333. Local © 021/6279-8888; fax 021/6279-8887. www.ritzcarlton.com/hotels/shanghai.

Sofitel Hyland Hotel
505 Nanjing Rd. East (Metro: Renmin Guangchang or He Nan Rd.)

The hotel is small and in one of the most fabulous locations in town—smack-dab in the middle of the shopping district. Prices are less than at other luxury hotels ($105 on a winter special); this hotel remains the secret find of many a visitor. I paid $200 for my room on the club floor, which offers many, many perks, making it worth the splurge. U.S. reservations © 800-SOFITEL. Local © 021/6351-5888. www.accorhotels.com/asia.

Sleeping in Pudong

Pudong Shangri-La
33 Fu Cheng Lu, Pudong (Metro: Lu Jia Zui)

The Shangri-La just works. It is not the fanciest hotel in town, or even in Pudong. But it's one of the best hotels in Shanghai because it serves both the tourist and the businessperson well. It's also next door to a shopping mall.

Shangri-La has some unusual extras, such as airport transfers, that can be included in your room rate and are very much worth the money. My room cost $179 on a promotional deal. Rooms with views of the Bund cost more than those without. U.S. reservations © **800/942-5050.** Local © **021/6882-8888.** www.shangri-la.com.

SOFITEL JIN JIANG ORIENTAL
889 Yangga Na Lu (Metro: Expo Center)

I originally booked this hotel because I confused Jin Jiang and Jing An and thus found myself in a brand-new, very tony hotel in the middle of a still-developing area. By 2010 this is expected to be the heart of Pudong; now it's to one side. But never mind. Also note that the name is often written "J. J. Oriental."

You do have to take taxis everywhere, but if you're mindful of traffic, a ride to Yuyuan Gardens is a mere $5. It's also easier to get to the airport from here than from the other side of town. Furthermore, prices were low (I got a winter promotional rate of $105), there's a shopping mall in the basement, and the club floor was luxe personified. My personal butler was a nice touch, and sitting in my bathtub next to a wall of windows overlooking Pudong was not bad, either.

This is a great hotel to know about when prices are crazy in town, which happens during big conventions and special events (such as Formula 1 racing). There's an ATM in the lobby. I'm hopeful there will soon be a shuttle bus to the nearby Lotus Centre. U.S. reservations © **800-SOFITEL.** Local © **021/5050-4888.** www.accorhotels.com.

DINING IN SHANGHAI

Shanghai is famous for its own style of cuisine (rather bland, actually), its **crabs** (in season in Nov), and its **pan-fried brown noodles.** I have not only become addicted to these noodles, but have now tasted them in enough places around town that I know where the best ones are. They are also one of those things that you can hardly ever go wrong with—while they do taste different at each place that makes them, they are still just noodles—good for kids, picky eaters, and the travel weary. Brown noodles are made on the street; I don't normally eat street food when I travel, but you may be tempted by the noodles.

Should you happen to be a street-food person, there are a few streets for wandering and eating your way to heaven . . . or somewhere. Check out **Wujiang Lu,** near the Shi Men Road Metro station. This is a strolling street—the first part is devoted to Western-style fast food, and the second part is for local diners who prefer the real thing. Chef Jean-Georges says his street food of choice comes from **Xiang Yang Road,** between Julu and Changle roads.

Shanghai has a growing reputation as the swinging spot in the Pacific Rim, and a lot of this is related to European-style dining. Shanghai could be in London, New York, or Paris.

Restaurant Concepts

THREE ON THE BUND
No. 3 The Bund, 3 Zhong Shan Dong Yi Rd., at Guang-dong Rd. (Metro: Renmin Guangchang)

About the address: The building is on the Bund, but the door is on Guangdong Road. About the concept: Until recently, the Bund was best seen in the opening scenes of *Empire of the Sun.* About 10 years ago, an Australian chef by way of Hong Kong opened M on the Bund, the first of the Western-style fusion-chic restaurants—and with a spectacular view. Now the concept has gone further, with the first Western-owned landmark building on the Bund, across the street from M on the Bund in a building that was once "the club" to local foreigners. It's been totally redone—the decor is stunning—with a handful of designer restaurants and the only Evian health and beauty spa this side of France. This is also home to a few stores, including two Armani shops and 3, a designer store on two levels that carries many Euro big names. Online: www.threeonthe bund.com.

Make a reservation for all of the restaurants:

LARIS: Perhaps this was the most exciting of my meals at Three on the Bund because I already knew the Jean-Georges concept so well from Market in Paris, one of my favorite restaurants. The chef here came from Paris, so there is some crossover in the fusion. Laris is David Laris's first name restaurant; he comes from Conran's big-name places in London and does Australian and Pacific Rim fusion contemporary, then serves you his homemade chocolates after dinner. © 021/6321-9922.

JEAN-GEORGES: I visited for lunch, which was a good insight into the fashion scene, but dinner is probably better—for the view and the dress-up version of the fashion scene. The food at either meal is sublime; the bar is a re-creation of the famed Long Bar of Shanghai's storied past—where each man had a position at the bar based on his status in the business world. © 021/6321-7733.

WHAMPOA CLUB: This is the Chinese restaurant of the group; I am over the moon for the private rooms for tea service. My lunch here was a tad too Chinese for me, but the place was full, and the locals loved it. The decor is gorgeous, the view sublime, and the food creative Shanghainese, by a chef who made his name in Singapore. With six you do *not* get egg roll. © 021/6321-3737.

NEW HEIGHTS: This is the bar, the cafe, the casual restaurant that includes the terrace—the "in" spot to see the view of the Bund and the river. © 021/6321-0909.

THE CUPOLA: Dinner à deux? This is marriage proposal central. The private dining room in the building's cupola has a view to die for. You ring for the waiter; otherwise, it's private. © 021/6321-1101.

XINTIANDI
Huai Hai Rd. East (Metro: Huang Pi Nan Rd.)

This is a destination, not a restaurant—it's sort of a theme park of great architecture, some stores, and many bars and restaurants. Surely a must for seeing what's hot. I'd suggest just wandering and picking a restaurant that appeals to you. Or you may prefer to bar-hop. If you're looking for addresses to check out, there's **Nooch,** 123 Xinye Lu (© 021/6386-1281), and **TMSK,** 11 Beili Lu (© 021/6326-2227), which is best as a bar or a lesson in design. The prices in all the restaurants are more in keeping with New York than China.

Last trip, we tested **Ye Shanghai,** 338 Huang Pi Nan Rd., North Block (© 021/6311-2323), which is long on local rep for both decor and delish. It did not knock my socks off, although the Shanghai steamed buns were exceptional. I got us lost looking for this restaurant—it is to the side of the development.

Museum Concepts

I screwed up on this, so there's a chance you will, too: Most museums have cafes, but the Shanghai Museum and the Shanghai Art Museum are two different places.

Kathleen5 is the talk of the town—a restaurant at the Shanghai Art Museum. The chef is American-raised Chinese, and this is her fifth restaurant since returning to Shanghai. For off-the-Bund dining, this is the place for taste, view, and new style, complete with a large terrace. There is a Western menu. Shanghai Art Museum, 325 Nanjing Rd. West, 5th floor (© 021/6327-2221; Metro: Renmin Guangchang or Shi Men Rd.).

Nearby is the **Shanghai Museum Café.** The modern cafe is on the ground floor and serves Western-style snacks. It's chic, clean, and convenient. Good bathrooms, too. Figure $15 per head without drinks. Shanghai Museum, 201 Renmin Da Dao (© 021/6372-3500; Metro: Renmin Guangchang).

Snack & Shop

If you're out sightseeing or shopping and want to know where to go for a simple lunch or a quick bite, here are a few of my regular choices. I also eat at McDonald's and, tempted as I am, avoid street stalls. When in doubt, I test a luxury hotel's coffee shop.

LAKE PAVILION TEAHOUSE
257 Yuyuan Lu, Yuyuan Gardens (no nearby Metro)

When you go to Yuyuan Gardens and see the teahouse in the center, you will invariably want to dine there. I can't tell you the whole deal because we went on a Sunday and were trying to beat crowds, so we were there at an odd hour and almost everything was odd. However, here goes: The type of tea you are served and the price are related to your location in the teahouse. Upstairs is better. There are set tea menus, but you get no cucumber sandwiches, just tiny eggs and bits of local nibbles. We saw people eating dim sum downstairs—they seemed to have brought in their dim sum from a nearby takeout place. We were not amused. About $10 per person without serious food. © 021/6355-8270.

OLD CHINA HAND READING ROOM
27 Shaoxing Rd. (no nearby Metro)

This will probably require a taxi ride and some effort. But it's really fun and possibly worth doing, especially for the ladies. The place is right out of a novel or a movie—a true English tearoom with chinoiserie edges for those wearing whalebone and toting stiff upper lips. Britannia rules the waves. Assam, m'dear? About $5 for a cuppa. © 021/6473-2526.

SUPER BRAND MALL FOOD COURT
Pudong (Metro: Lu Jia Zui)

Don't confuse the food court on the fifth floor of the Super Brand Mall with the mini food court in the basement at the entrance to Lotus Centre. The food court has many of the usual Western suspects as well as a cute fast-food Thai place, which will set you back less than $10 per head, with beer.

SHOPPING SHANGHAI

Stores in Shanghai are an incredible jumble of styles; few were what I was expecting. In short, there's plenty of Western style while communist-era shops are disappearing. Shanghai has a far greater rep for trendiness than Beijing—there's lots of fashion, from Euro name brands to Chinese no-names. This is the place to shop for clothing, especially for teens, tweens, and others in need of the latest thing.

The flea markets (there are several) are pure heaven; the museum stores are also good—especially the one at the Shanghai Museum. Most hotels have shops; prices in hotel gift shops are always higher than elsewhere, but at least you don't have to deal with crazy salespeople or bargaining techniques.

Shanghai Home Style

Ah, Shanghai style, that design category in home furnishings—and a little bit in fashion—that conjures up the 1930s and the days of drugs and jazz and decadence in the foreign concessions of old Shanghai. David Tang capitalized on this style enormously when he created his **Shanghai Tang** stores, but the look is in movies and hotel lobbies and dreams of pearl-shaped silk lampshades and overstuffed easy chairs and girls in tight-tight dresses selling cigarettes and maybe themselves.

There was romance in 1930s Shanghai style, but few in Shanghai have looked backward for inspiration. David Tang has used it in his Shanghai Tang stores and his private China Clubs. **Xintiandi** (p. 210), created from ancient stone buildings, reflects an entirely different kind of urban reclamation and old-fashioned Shanghai style. There is a Shanghai Tang store in Xintiandi.

Aaron's Turn

One of the things that makes shopping in China so unbelievably great is the all-out, excessive bargaining. Honestly, you will buy things you didn't even want just because you got caught up in the excitement of the bargaining process.

I became the King of Bargaining because of my take-no-prisoners attitude. I was cheated on my first shopping adventures and terribly upset because I was dumb. After that, I felt compelled to make up all that I had overpaid. At the time of my first shopping/bargaining foray, I was convinced that I was making out like a bandit—however it is that bandits make out. It wasn't until later that I added up all the prices and realized that I could have bought the same stuff for the same price at Wal-Mart. After that, I honed my skills and managed to buy twice the amount of merchandise for half the price.

I try to be polite, I don't criticize the merchandise, but I like to pay 12% to 25% of the asking price. I tell the vendors I'm poor, I'm a student, I don't have that kind of money, and I know they are offering tourist prices.

The important thing is to not let them know that you are too interested. In fact, it works better if there are two of you to play good cop–bad cop—or, in this case, good shop–bad shop. For instance, you examine the item and get an initial price from the vendor. The bad cop friend says, "No way, man. You don't really want that, and it's waaaay too expensive."

The vendor jumps in and lowers the price. It's very important at this point that you express genuine interest, that the vendor knows you will buy when you can agree on a price. He has to understand, as the old Chinese proverb goes, a duck in the hand is better than no ducks in Peking. Once they know you will buy, all they have to do is close the sale, which is a matter of price.

The biggest problem is that the prices you are quoted at first are good prices compared to those we are used to in America. It's just that these are very high prices for China and for the quality of the merchandise.

Brand Awareness

Duties on foreign-made merchandise are incredibly high, so brand-name goods sold in China have never offered any value. Although all brands are now available in Shanghai, even Hong Kong is cheaper for such items. In fact, many say that Hong Kong has survived the latest financial downturn because the wealthy Chinese come to shop.

We all know that China is expected to be the world's largest consumer market. With Shanghai considered a more fashion-motivated city than Beijing, most brands have tried to break into the Shanghai market. The brands already established in both cities often say they have better customers in Beijing and that Shanghai shoppers are too picky.

More and more luxe malls have opened in Shanghai; the world's largest Louis Vuitton store has arrived. Phew. Cartier has just opened on the Bund, thankfully next door to a bank, which you can rob before shopping. I think we should all be learning the Chinese brands, but the shopping ops are more and more oriented toward Western brands. Go figure.

Money Matters

See the "Money Matters" section in chapter 2 for a complete discussion of money in China. ATMs are readily available. You should bargain in all markets.

Tipping Tips

As you all remember from Communism 101, which we were taught in high school near our bomb shelters, Communists do not believe in tipping. At one point, tipping was almost illegal; then it was merely frowned upon. Now it seems to be frowned upon by expats who don't want you to ruin the system because they have been getting by without tipping. Tourists do indeed tip. In fact, the best way to teach capitalism is to prove that it works; that is not done with a lecture, but with a tip. I tip everyone, and I tip big time for work well done.

Note: The Okura Garden Hotel has signs everywhere asking you not to tip. Elsewhere, you can tip in U.S. dollars.

Shipping Tips

DHL: The company has a comprehensive shipping network throughout China and Hong Kong. For Express Centre locations, call © **021/6536-2900** or search www.cn.dhl.com.

UPS Shanghai: To find shipping locations or to arrange for pickup, call © **021/6391-5555** or visit www.ups.com/asia/cn/using/services/locate/englocate.html.

Best Market Day in Shanghai

Dong Jia Du Fabric Market
Dong Jia Du Rd. (no nearby Metro)

Combine this with a visit to the nearby flea market at Dong Tai for 1 perfect day in Shanghai. Otherwise, just plow in and watch your dreams come true. This is an indoor market, with open stalls and tables laden with fabrics. Tailors lurk in the side shops, and some of the fabric vendors have goods already made up. My best buy of my last visit came from this market: embroidered shawls for $5 each.

5 Best Stores in Shanghai

Each of these stores is described in the Resources portion of this chapter.

Hu & Hu
1685 Wuzhong Lu (no nearby Metro)

Out in the boonies a bit, but worth it if you are looking for antiques, mostly restored. This villagelike warehouse has incredible home style, and the owner speaks American English. Have your taxi wait. There are other similar stores (not as good, to my eye) in the area.

LOTUS CENTRE
Super Brand Mall, Pudong (Metro: Lu Jia Zui)

Attention, Kmart shoppers! This grocery center and hyper-marché is inside a mall. You can skip the mall and just take the escalator downstairs to the groceries. Once inside the grocery store, take the interior beltway upstairs to the next level for clothes, dry goods, electronics, DVDs, and so forth. You must pay cash unless your Visa card is from a Chinese bank (ha).

SHANGHAI MUSEUM GIFT SHOP
201 Renmin Da Dao, People's Square (Metro: Renmin Guangchang)

You can get into the shop without going into the museum, although why you would do that is something only I under-stand. There's everything from books to gift wrap, to repro-ductions of items from the museum collections. Silk scarves, porcelain, postcards, calligraphy. You get the gist.

SUCHOW COBBLER
17 Fuchow Rd. (Metro: He Nan Rd.)

The world's tiniest store, right off the Bund, sells embroidered slippers in Chinese styles that have been Westernized to the point of high chic.

W. W. CHAN TAILOR & SON LTD.
129A Mao Ming Rd. (Metro: Shi Men Rd.)

The best tailors in Hong Kong have traditionally been from Shaghai families who fled in 1949. Now they are beginning to come back to serve the new China. W. W. Chan is one such tailor—one of the big two in Hong Kong.

There's a shop in the Shanghai Hilton as well as this free-standing store across the street from the Okura Garden Hotel off Huai Hai Road. Men's suits, shirts, ties, and such. Prices are about 20% less than in Hong Kong. You will pay about $600 for a custom-tailored suit.

Company representatives visit the U.S. twice a year.

Shanghai Shopping Neighborhoods

PUDONG

Pudong isn't really a neighborhood; it's a city—a big city with many neighborhoods. It is sometimes written "Putong" in the old-fashioned form.

To further confuse you, the business district of Pudong is called Lu Jia Zui; the Stock Exchange is here, as are many main offices of the big banks, the Jin Mao Tower, the Shangri-La Hotel, and, of course, the Pearl TV Tower. In short, tourists call it Pudong and some business guys call it Lu Jia Zui, but they are the same destination.

Pudong has changed so much that there's not much I can tell you that will remain accurate. Whether you choose to stay in this part of town or not, you must, must, must come over and get a view of the Bund at night. And don't forget the brown noodles. Or the **Lotus Centre,** which is in the Super Brand Mall.

To see what's happening, you want the area nestled between the river and the Pearl TV Tower. The rest is just there. This can be done in a drive-by, and then you can explore the mall on foot.

THE BUND

Located on a bend in the Huangpu River, the Bund is enhanced by the river's natural curve. It is called *Waitan* in Chinese. There are buildings on one side of the waterfront, then comes the part for cars (some call this a street), and then, right alongside the quayside, there's a large boardwalk so that one can promenade along the river. Yes, there are guys with cameras who will take your picture for a small fee; it's just like Atlantic City. This is not a great shopping street, but it is changing, and Armani has arrived. The side streets jutting away from the river right off the Bund are the ones to watch, starting with Fuchow Street.

NANJING ROAD

Perhaps the most famous street in Shanghai after the Bund, Nanjing Road (p. 219) is also the city's main shopping drag, despite its enormous length (over 10km/6¼ miles). Much of the main shopping district is a pedestrian mall. Don't miss this at night—stores are open until 9 or 10pm. If you plan to have a stroll to see a good bit of this famous street, begin at the Bund and the Peace Hotel. After a few banks and hotels, after you cross Shanxi Road, you'll be in the heart of the pedestrian mall and shopping greats. This is the eastern part of Nanjing Road. It is not really within walking distance of the western portion of Nanjing Road.

In the eastern district, you'll find everything from silk shops to TTs (tourist traps), to pearl shops, to stores that specialize in gadgets and others for sports equipment to wannabe Jing Maos. There's Western style, Eastern style, and no style whatsoever. But plenty of McDonald's and lotsa bright lights.

HUAI HAI ROAD

If you care about your sanity, avoid Huai Hai Road (formerly Ave. Joffre to the French, and also written Weihai Rd.) on Saturday. This is the main drag of the fashionable French concession and the high street for local fashionistas aged 20 to 30. Most of the stores are either big-name global brands or Chinese inspirations—copies of European trends selling at low Chinese prices, with equally low quality. In the crowd, I began to experience strange psychological reactions to my immediate world. I sank into Chinese philosophy, suddenly feeling very small, very insignificant, and very stupid for having thought I mattered. In no time at all, you can have a Huai Hai headache.

Note: Do a drive-by in a taxi first to find the parts you want to explore on foot. Not only is the street very long, but it also

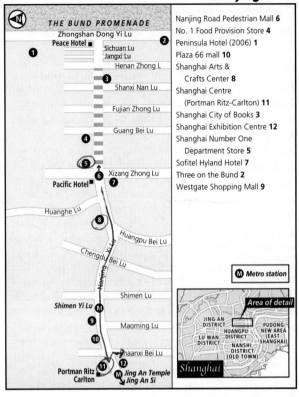

THE BUND PROMENADE

Zhongshan Dong Yi Lu

Peace Hotel ■

Sichuan Lu
Jiangxi Lu

Henan Zhong L.

Shanxi Nan Lu

Fujian Zhong Lu

Guang Bei Lu

Xizang Zhong Lu

Pacific Hotel ■

Huanghe Lu

Huangpu Bei Lu

Chengdu Bei Lu

Shimen Lu

Shimen Yi Lu

Maoming Lu

Shaanxi Bei Lu

Portman Ritz
Carlton

Jing An Temple
Jing An Si

Nanjing Road Pedestrian Mall 6
No. 1 Food Provision Store 4
Peninsula Hotel (2006) 1
Plaza 66 mall 10
Shanghai Arts &
   Crafts Center 8
Shanghai Centre
   (Portman Ritz-Carlton) 11
Shanghai City of Books 3
Shanghai Exhibition Centre 12
Shanghai Number One
   Department Store 5
Sofitel Hyland Hotel 7
Three on the Bund 2
Westgate Shopping Mall 9

M *Metro station*

Area of detail

JING AN
DISTRICT

HUANGPU
DISTRICT

PUDONG
NEW AREA
(EAST
SHANGHAI)

LU WAN
DISTRICT

NANSHI
DISTRICT
(OLD TOWN)

Shanghai

has east and west portions. The western portion has the shops you will be most interested in; the eastern portion is just now getting it together.

Also note: There was a junk market for clothes and designer (well, fake designer) merchandise on Huai Hai Road at Xiangyang Road, but it is closing and may already be gone by the time you read this. This market has relocated twice since I've known it, and it will surely pop up someplace else. Ask around.

Jenny's Turn: Introducing Changle Road

While staying at the Okura Garden Hotel, I decided to take advantage of the fact that the famed **Huai Hai Road** was a block away. This bustling street of consumerism has the reputation of being the "it" road for shopping in Shanghai. What I found was the same old Western and global stores you find at home . . . and way too many people.

There were crowds, bad attitudes, and much shoving and pushing—and that was just in Starbucks. I was quickly losing my sanity. Luckily, on the way back to the hotel, I discovered **Changle Road,** a street that anyone could fall in love with. This smaller, less busy street not only runs east and west, but sells East and West style-wise. It parallels Huai Hai Road on a map, but it is much more than a parallel universe.

The atmosphere and merchandise in half the shops was funky and trendy—think Greenwich Village in New York or Melrose Avenue in LA. The rest of the stores have high-quality, traditional Chinese merchandise—both fashion and accessories. This street is perfect for both the young and the hip or the older and more sophisticated.

More important, Changle Road has it all, without lines, crowds, or pushy people. The street is as long as Huai Hai Road, and the best shopping parts are near the Okura Garden Hotel. There's no bargaining, but prices are more than fair.

JING AN

The Portman Ritz-Carlton, the Four Seasons, the JC Mandarin, and many, many other hotels—and a few shopping malls—are in this part of town. It includes West Nanjing Road and the Shanghai Exhibition Centre, which is across the street from the Portman Ritz-Carlton.

This is not much of a funky shopping district, although it has a big mall, **Westgate;** several other malls are building up around here, such as the new **Plaza 66.**

This part of town is also called Nanjing Road West because the far-reaching Nanjing Road comes up here, but it is not the same animal as the Nanjing Road you will learn to love in the center of town near the Sofitel Hyland Hotel.

Xintiandi

I have mistakenly been calling this Xanadu, partly because I can pronounce it and partly because of the poem. Xintiandi also has to do with Marco Polo or Kubla Kahn or something like that. But pay me no heed; just taxi on over here at least once, and surely for a meal—it's especially nice at night, and the stores are open 'til about 10pm.

Xintiandi is in the French concession and resembles a film set or an American festival marketplace, although it was built with Hong Kong money. It is said to be a restoration of old houses, converted to stores and restaurants. The feel is nothing like Colonial Williamsburg or even Disney, but is wall-to-wall charm with tons of hot design looks in the use of tiles, inventive seating, and unusual light fixtures. In short, this is a village of cutting-edge chic.

This complex—a true must-do—is at the eastern end of Huai Hai Road, a part of town where redevelopment began only recently. Office buildings have arrived; luxury housing is expected soon. The bars are downright inspirational, from a design point of view.

Old City

This is the name most often given to the oldest part of town, which is also known as **Nanshi**. This was the Chinese city in the days of the foreign concessions. It was walled many years ago. It is quickly being torn down and replaced with the New China, but some quaint winding roads, alleys, and tin shanties remain to fill you with glee.

Also here are the **Yuyuan Gardens**, a Disney-meets-China-town parcel of land with buildings and gardens, a teahouse, a temple, a market, and antiques stores. It's the city's number-one tourist attraction—and for good reason, although I am sick at just how touristy this area has become.

The Old City is also home to the **Dong Tai Antiques Market,** which feels a lot more authentic than just about any other part of town. Nearby is the **Dong Jia Du,** the fabric market (p. 228)—which may be my favorite shopping space in Shanghai.

HONG QIAO

This area includes the Hong Qiao International Airport, many furniture and antiques warehouses, a mall or two, and huge gated communities where wealthy expats live in either modern high-rises or town houses organized as village developments. Even though traffic can be fierce, if you have any interest in furniture, you won't want to miss this district. Get a taxi to stay with you and wait as you shop.

SHANGHAI RESOURCES A TO Z

....

Note: If you don't find listings here that are mentioned in other guidebooks, there could be a good reason. Maybe they are gone, or maybe I didn't think them worth your time, or maybe something else happened . . ..

Antique Furniture

See "Furniture" section, p. 230.

Antiques

MINGYUAN ANTIQUES STORE
Cui Xiu Hall at Big Rockery, Shanghai Yu, Yuyuan Gardens (no nearby Metro)

This store is expensive, but it has excellent stuff. Note that it is inside the garden part of Yuyuan Gardens, which you must pay to enter.

SHANGHAI MUSEUM ANTIQUES SHOP
Shanghai Museum, 16 Henan Lu (Metro: Renmin Guangchang)

Not to be confused with the downstairs gift shop, this is an upstairs shop, maybe 72 sq. m (775 sq. ft.), of expensive but government-approved antiques. Everything is behind glass, and it looks much like an exhibition. Lots of little teapots, lots of high prices.

Antiques Markets

If you go to Shanghai for one shopping experience, it has to be for buying antiques, both small decorative pieces and furniture. The antiques markets are heaven, and the prices are so low you will want to weep. There are also good markets in Beijing, so don't blow your wad. Remember, most of this stuff is fake; trust no one. But if you see any more of those pewter and ceramic bowls, get me a few, please.

DONG TAI MARKET
Dong Tai Lu (no nearby Metro)

This is one of my favorite addresses in Shanghai, where I want to buy out all of the stalls. An outdoorsy type of thing, the market is not particularly large and takes place on just two perpendicular streets. The vendors sell from wagons or little trailers; there are a few shops. Not too many dealers speak English, but I didn't find that to be a problem.

Whatever you do, the first time you fall in love with an item, price it but don't buy. You tend to see a lot of similar things, and prices can vary dramatically—even without bargaining. I almost bought a set of three blue-and-white ceramic men for $100. I figured I could get them for $50 and liked the idea a whole lot. I didn't do it because they were hard to pack. Days later I found them, priced at $50 for the set of three, at a fancy hotel gift shop. The market price should have been $30!

FANG BANG MARKET/SHANGHAI OLD STREET
Henan Nan Lu and Fuxing Zhong Lu/Fang Bang Zhong Lu
(no nearby Metro)

Shanghai Old Street is a very commercial section that looks almost like a festival marketplace from a bad American mall, with carts in the street and vendors selling baskets and kites. The closer you get to Henan Lu (and the farther from Yuyuan), the more it turns into something that feels like an authentic neighborhood. Finally you get to a dumpy little building that will surely be condemned soon. This is the home of the Fang Bang Market.

On weekends there are antiques in the street and more dealers sitting on the curbs bearing tote bags crammed with hot or fake (or both) Ming vases that they will try to entice you to buy.

The market takes place every day. *But* it's not very good on weekdays, when only about 30% of the vendors show up. On weekends, especially Sunday, it is crammed and quite the scene.

To get here, I'd suggest a taxi to the Henan Nan Lu side (after 11am on weekdays, 9am on weekends). Or walk from the Haobao Building (see below). Look for rather touristy torii gates and a pedestrian shopping street. Before your eye can figure out which part is real and which is stagecraft, you see the dealers and spy the heaps of delicious junk, on the curbs and falling out of stalls and tiny shops. They're to your left if your back is to the torii gate and Henan Road.

HAOBAO BUILDING
Yuyuan Gardens

Many people don't even know there is an antiques mart within the "village" of the gardens, or another one a few blocks away. This market has changed in recent years and now leans toward the Tibetan.

The prices on antique silk garments and other items here are so low that I became giddy on my first trip; I touched and tried everything from padded silk jackets in dusty mauve to small embroidered pockets (popular because Chinese clothes do not come with pockets).

Bargain like mad. Many dealers speak English.

Arts & Crafts

LIFESTYLE FURNITURE
17 Fuzhou Rd. (Metro: Renmin Guangchang)

This furniture store has mostly ceramics, including many pieces created with photos of Old Shanghai. Most stunning: the coffee mugs with silk tassels. Suzhou Cobblers (see previous listing) is at the same address but up a different stoop.

SHANGHAI ARTS & CRAFTS CENTER
190–208 Nanjing Rd. East (Metro: He Nan Rd.)

Four floors of fun—every type of craft product you can imagine is sold here, including silk by the bolt and all sorts of silk products. I bought printed silk scarves and cut-velvet silk scarves. The pajamas were rather expensive; no one at home would ever believe you paid that much ($85–$100) for them.

SUZHOU COBBLERS
17 Fuzhou Rd. (Metro: Renmin Guangchang)

Right off the Bund near Jardin de le Sens, this is the cutest little store in Shanghai. It sells amazing embroidered shoes of a quality far above souvenir slippers, and the designs employ modern motifs. My favorites were green satin with bok choy dancing across the toes. Prices are about $50 per pair. Horribly chic; an undeniable must-have.

Books

If you stroll the midsection of Fuzhou Lu, on what was once called Culture Street, you will find an entire street of Chinese booksellers.

Booze

Look in the "Foodstuffs" listings below for large food emporiums; the ones that have liquor departments usually sell specialty wines that incorporate dead mice, snakes, and so on, or are made with parts of animal bodies. I bought superchef Alain Ducasse seal-penis wine for his birthday.

You will pay top yuan for international brands of booze, but local brands are inexpensive. Ones with snakes in them do cost more.

Chinese Style

SHANGHAI TANG
Jin Jang Hotel, 59 Mao Ming Rd. (Metro: Shi Men Rd.), and Xintiandi, 15 North Block, 181 Tai Cang Rd. (no nearby Metro)

The selection here is not as good as in Hong Kong. The style is fabulous, but the prices are high. Check out the cashmere Mao sweaters.

ZHANG'S TEXTILES
Shanghai Centre, Nanjing Xi Lu (Metro: Jiang An Temple)

Antique textiles for collectors. The most famous dealer in China, Zhang's also does business in Beijing.

Department Stores

SHANGHAI NUMBER ONE DEPARTMENT STORE
830 Nanjing Rd. (Metro: Renmin Guangchang)

Number One Department Store is one of the most famous, old-timey communist-era Chinese department stores. It's at the beginning (or end) of the commercial part of Nanjing Road, right near Renmin Park where Nanjing Road changes from eastern direction to western. Now it sells Chanel makeup; how the world changes.

ISETAN
1038 Nanjing Xi Lu West (Metro: Jing An Temple)

This branch of Isetan is about 1 block from the Portman Ritz-Carlton in a modern, Western-style mall that was recently remodeled and filled with big-name stores. Isetan is a Japanese department store known for younger brands, kickier fashions, and lower prices than some of the other Japanese department stores. Not only does it carry an international lineup of brands, but many names (such as Michel Klein) do specialty lines, and there are many super brands you just haven't ever seen before. Large sizes need not apply.

MAISON MODE
1312 Huai Hai Rd. West (Metro: Shi Men Rd.)

Possibly the classiest department store in town, the upscale Maison Mode carries fancy Western brands such as Ferragamo.

YUYUAN DEPARTMENT STORE
Yuyuan Gardens (no nearby Metro)

I discovered this department store by accident while shopping at the downstairs flea market. This is sort of a smaller and classier version of Number One. It not only has a good fabric department, but the staff actually bargained with me while the salesgirls fought each other for my business. I paid $12 per meter for silk *dévoré* (cut velvet).

Designers

European designer stores are popping up everywhere, especially in hotel lobbies and big, fat malls. Prices are at least 20% more than in Hong Kong and may be even higher compared to your local mall in Hometown, USA. Did you really come to China to see Louis Vuitton? Plaza 66 has most of the French big names; Cartier is on the Bund.

Drugstores

WATSON'S, THE CHEMIST
Huai Hai Rd. West (no nearby Metro)

Watson's is one of my favorite stores in Hong Kong, so it's no surprise that I love it in Shanghai. I can spend a few minutes each day loading up on candy bars and soft drinks, health and beauty products, medicines, and gadgets. Avoid U.S.- and European-brand makeup and fragrances, which are stunningly expensive. I've bought many marvelous (read: cheap) gifts here for my $3 friends. The gifts look like they are worth at least $5, maybe more.

DVDs

Most locals buy pirated DVDs from favorite sources that come and go like the wind—for good reason. The action is mostly at night. You will be approached if you promenade on Nanjing Road after dark.

I like legal DVDs from **Shanghai City of Books,** 345 Nanjing Rd. There is usually someone on staff who speaks enough English to tell you if the disc you favor is in English.

Fabrics

DONG JIA DU FABRIC MARKET
Dong Jia Du Rd. at Zhong Shan Rd. (no nearby Metro)

You have to like markets, you have to like fabric, and you should know your stuff. If you said yes to at least two of those three points, welcome to heaven. This large market is filled with stalls selling fabrics; there are also tailors. Some of the stalls stock simple ready-made items. My best buy was an embroidered fabric stole for $5. The same embroidered fabric costs $75 a meter in Paris and $20 a meter in this market. Need I say more? The tricky part: In shirt fabrics, you are looking at local Chinese cottons, not European goods. Don't believe your tailor unless he can prove he uses imported fabric.

Silk King
819 Nanjing Xi Lu (Metro: He Nan Rd.), and other locations

The stores in this chain vary with the location. They are easy to shop; usually at least one salesperson speaks English. Prices are higher than in the fabric market, but the store is almost Western in style.

Zhang Yan Juan
Wife Ding Cloth Store, 438 Fang Bang Zhong Lu (no nearby Metro)

This store is part of a development called Old Shanghai Street, which I adore. The store features only fabric and items made of the fabric in the homespun blue cloth of the Henan region of China. For blue-and-white freaks, this is really a find.

Fakes

The fakes market in Shanghai isn't nearly as good—or as much fun—as Beijing's. Still, you might want to stop by for a few giggles or inexpensive gifts and souvenirs. But the best-known market was just torn down. A new market will surely pop up. Ask your hotel concierge.

Foodstuffs

Lotus Centre
Super Brand Mall, Pudong (Metro: Lu Jia Zui)

This is my hypermarché and grocery of choice. It has one floor of groceries and one floor of dry goods. I won't get into the story of the day I went to buy a bra and the saleswoman decided to help fit me—over my clothes.

No. 1 Food Provision Store
720 Nanjing Rd. East (Metro: Renmin Guangchang)

This just might be my favorite store in Shanghai. It is on the pedestrian mall part of Nanjing Road and is open in the evening, so you can go here on a nighttime stroll. The store is large, in the colonial European architectural style, but only two stories high.

The ground floor sells fresh produce, dried fruit, liquor, and gift baskets. It's Harrods Food Hall come to Shanghai. All signs are in Chinese (no pinyin, even). Upstairs there's a supermarket.

No. 2 Food Provision Store
887 Huai Hai Rd. West (Metro: Shan Xi Nan Rd.)

This store is smaller than No. 1 Food Provision Store, not nearly as much fun and somewhat ruined by the enormous KFC sign out front. It's worth a visit if you are strolling this part of Huai Hai Road and haven't been spoiled by No. 1.

Furniture

There are so many furniture warehouses in Shanghai that you will go nuts with greed and desire (at least, I did). In terms of bargaining on final price and making shipping arrangements, it's easiest to give all your business to one dealer.

You'll pass many furniture warehouses as you drive into town from the Hong Qiao Airport—Hong Qiao is the main district for antique furniture warehouses, but not the only one.

Note that many an expat has taken the furniture back to a different climate in the United States, only to have it crack during the first winter. Consider buying a humidifier once in the U.S.

Also, a true story: I bought a piece of rustic-style chinoiserie at Galeries Lafayette in Paris (for my Paris apartment) for $600, delivery and taxes included. It turned out to be a better deal than shipping from Shanghai, although the piece bought in China would have cost only $200 to $250.

If you plan to ship your purchases, consider several factors. Prices on shipping are not that high, and you will be impressed. However, prices on clearing goods through a Customs broker and trucking from the port of entry may be obscene. I paid

$125 to ship a piece and an additional $425 to have it delivered, a mere 161km (100 miles) from the port of entry.

And speaking of money: While I found prices in Shanghai laughably inexpensive, dealers say that outside of town there are warehouses that are even cheaper, such as **Nineteen Town,** 19 Jin Xin Lu, Jiu Ting. Needless to say, the farther off the beaten path you wander, the more you need a translator.

G-E TANG ANTIQUES
7 Hu Qing Ping Hwy. (no nearby Metro)

This establishment is extremely tourist oriented; it has a website (www.getang.com), advertises in the city's freebie tourist map, and has a reputation among visitors and expats. There's even a most impressive English-language brochure.

The shop is very chic and sleek; the young men who work here are dressed in black T-shirts and black trousers, and could have stepped out of an Armani showroom. Many speak English. The goods are gorgeous.

Too gorgeous (and too expensive) for my taste. I found the whole setup very touristy and bordering on offensive. I cannot find anyone who agrees with me. I asked the staff to show me the junk and was led to a warehouse of unrestored furniture in the rear. This was much more fun. I was quoted various prices for the same piece—as is, cleaned up, or restored.

Shipping usually doubles the cost, so a painted blanket chest (maybe it was a tea chest?) or a set of drawers would end up being $700 to $1,000 when shipped to the United States. Having seen the quality of the pieces before they were restored, I simply didn't think they were worth it.

The place is very seductive—and a good starting point as you learn what you want and what you want to spend.

HENRY ANTIQUE WAREHOUSE
8 Hong Zhou Lu (no nearby Metro)

This one is a little tricky, so don't pay too much attention to what you think the sign says or is pointing to. Henry is not in the modern building in front of you, but in a low-slung warehouse down a dead-end street alongside that modern building.

This is a huge showroom where everyone speaks English and people are buying as if there is no tomorrow. There are more than 2,000 pieces of furniture on hand. Yes, they have been restored. The warehouse is not far from Hu & Hu (see below). E-mail: henryantique@eastday.com.

HU & HU ANTIQUES
1685 Wuzhong Lu (no nearby Metro)

This store is not far from the Hong Qiao warehouse district, but not really in it, either. The nearby area has blossomed lately, and you will go mad with greed.

Hu & Hu is the rage of town and everyone's favorite shop; certainly, it was one of my most fantastic shopping experiences in all my years of doing *Born to Shop*—and I didn't buy a thing.

First off, one of the Hus is a young woman named Marybelle Hu who is American-born Chinese (ABC), attended Smith College, and has since come back to China. I hope she gets into politics and becomes president, or whatever they have—emperor? Needless to say, her English is flawless, her organizational skills are amazing, and the store functions like a professional New York showroom. I haven't ever seen anything like this in China.

The warehouse is a warehouse—modern, not crammed or dirty and dusty. The concrete courtyard is for cars and taxis; an old wagon filled with flowers was a stunning decorative touch. They sure have a handle on style here.

For information or even photos online, e-mail hu-hu@online.sh.cn.

ZHONG ZHONG JIA YUAN
3050 He Chuan Rd. (no nearby Metro)

Located between Hu & Hu and Henry, this large warehouse is done up in a series of room sets. Someone speaks English, there is a large selection, and, yes, the company ships. In fact, it offers detailed information on various sizes of containers. Hours are daily from 9am until 10pm.

Malls

BUND 18
18 the Bund (Metro: Renmin Guangchang)

This isn't really a mall any more than Three on the Bund is a mall—it's a similar restaurant and retail complex that houses the restaurant created by the Pourcel twins (three-star French chefs) and the snazzy new **Cartier** shop, as well as other designer shops.

JING JANG DICKSON CENTRE
400 Changle Rd. (Metro: Shi Men Rd.)

The fanciest and most upscale Western mall in Shanghai is owned by the same businessman who owns Harvey Nichols in London. The mall is so chic it doesn't open until 11am (but it stays open until 9pm). Most of the really big-name shops, including Ralph Lauren, Lalique, and so on, are in this mall, which is the kingpin of the Huai Hai Road shopping district. The building is new but done up like redbrick-goes-Art-Deco. If you haven't already guessed, there are no bargains on designer goods in China because the import taxes are outrageously high. The stores are mostly empty and the help is very cool, probably terrified you will require them to speak English.

MAO MING CENTRE
Mao Ming Rd. at Changle Rd. (Metro: Shi Men Rd.)

This luxury mall is right near the Dickson Centre and across the street from the Okura Garden Hotel. It boasts the usual Western suspects.

Plaza 66
1266 Nanjing Xi Lu (Metro: Jing An Temple)

Yawn, another fancy mall with big, big, big Euro names. Here's the largest Louis Vuitton store in the world, along with brands like Chanel, Dior, and Escada. You get the picture.

Shanghai Centre
Nanjing Xi Lu (Metro: Jing An Temple)

This is not a traditional mall, but a multiuse center with a hotel, an apartment block, and various stores. It has a brand-new Gucci, a Ferragamo, a Starbucks, and so on.

Super Brand Mall
Pudong (Metro: Lu Jia Zui)

The mall was not quite ready for prime time on my recent visits, but the **Lotus Centre** was bustling, and I had a ball. We also had good fun in the food court on the seventh floor; try the Thai fast-food place. The best way to get here is to walk from the Shangri-La Hotel next door, or take the Metro or a ferry to Pudong.

Lotus is much like Auchan, a French hypermarché—a two-level store that is supermarket on one level and sells dry goods on the other. Can you believe I didn't buy Jenny a down coat for $10? This is a great place to buy telephones and small electronics. You may also have fun with foodstuffs—aside from the inscrutable, you will find brands you know in flavors created for the local market. Lays Beijing duck–flavor potato chips were one of my faves.

Times Square
93–99 Huai Hai Rd. East (Metro: Renmin Guangchang)

The first mainland China branch of the mall that changed a portion of Hong Kong's shopping style. It's a youth-oriented mall with name brands and attitude—but wait, it has a branch of my favorite supermarket, City Super.

Aaron's Turn: Sneak Me Some Feet

I saw some amazing shoes in China. I'm "big" on Puma and the Adidas-Kick brand. In China, I saw lots of cool designs that aren't available in the States. One pair of blue Adidas will forever be the pair that got away; it was pure love. Alas, I have size 13 (American) feet, and the largest pair of shoes I saw in China was size 10. And these were considered something of a novelty.

I was so depressed about having to leave stores without shoes that I actually starting taking pictures of the shoes I couldn't have. Talk about desperation. I would have been totally depressed except I kept thinking about Houston Rockets center Yao Ming. If I couldn't find a fit, where does he get his shoes?

WESTGATE SHOPPING MALL
1038 Nanjing Xi Lu (Metro: Jing An Temple)

I like this mall because it's 1 block from the Portman Ritz-Carlton, across the street from the JC Mandarin, and near the Four Seasons Hotel. It's very Western, and it has a branch of Isetan, the Japanese department store—and a branch of everything else, too.

Pearls

If you are going on to Beijing, I suggest you wait for the Pearl Market there. Otherwise, have a look at **Pearl City**, 558 Nanjing Rd. East, a mini-mall of dealers.

Supermarkets

NO. 1 FOOD PROVISION STORE
720 Nanjing Rd. East (Metro: Renmin Guangchang)

There's a supermarket upstairs. See p. 229.

PARK 'N SHOP
Westgate Mall (Metro: Jing An Temple), and other locations

Another Hong Kong supermarket chain; this branch is near the Portman Ritz-Carlton.

WELLCOME
Shanghai Centre, Portman Ritz-Carlton hotel, Nanjing Rd. (Metro: Jing An Temple)

I'm not certain if you would make a special trip here just for the Wellcome, but boy, was I excited to find it. Its Hong Kong–style supermarket luxury was a welcome comfort after too many dog days on the streets, and I was happy to load up on snacks and my favorite fiber cereal.

Tailors

Before the communist takeover, Shanghai was famous for its community of tailors. Most of them left in the late 1940s and re-established themselves in Hong Kong. Now the trend is reversing.

W. W. CHAN & SONS TAILOR LTD.
Shanghai Hilton, 250 Hua Shan Rd. (Metro: Jing An Temple or Chang Shu Rd.); 129A-2 Mao Ming Rd. (Metro: Shi Men Rd.)

Peter Chan's family is from Shanghai; he was born in Hong Kong and was the first Hong Kong tailor to return to Shanghai. One of his shops is in the lobby of the Hilton; the other is directly across from the Okura Garden Hotel right off Huai Hai Road. He specializes in men's clothing. Prices are approximately 20% less than in Hong Kong. To make an appointment prior to arrival, e-mail sales@wwchan.com or call ✆ 021/ 6248-2768.

Tea

There are a few tea markets for locals, but they are far out and you will need a local guide or interpreter. The best-known market, **Tian San ChaCha**, is in Hongqiao. (*Cha* is "tea" in Chinese.)

Start your quest at Three on the Bund, which has a tea sommelier and 80 different kinds of tea.

All grocery stores and Chinese herbal shops sell tea.

Teens

A walk along Huai Hai Road is all you need to see more shops of young fashions than your brain can compute. Also see Jenny's report on p. 220.

UNIQLO
333 Nanjing Rd. East (Metro: Han Zhong Rd.)

This is a Japanese fashion supermarket, something like the Gap with simple and classic must-haves, such as T-shirts in good colors and other basics. To get here, you go up a tube-enclosed escalator. This store is near the Sofitel Hyland Hotel.

Wedding Photos

Although there are wedding-photo salons in Beijing, the ones in Shanghai are better and much more fun. I will not name specific addresses, but I'll point you in the right direction so you can stare, or dare. Head to Huai Hai Road, in the thick of the French concession.

With China evolving into a Western consumer market, nothing is more valuable than a Western-style wedding or wedding photo. Because few can afford the real thing, there are zillions of salons where the bride and groom go for the day to be made over and photographed. Hair, makeup, and clothes are provided; you just say "cheese."

I was tempted to do this many times but figured that no wedding dress would ever fit me . . . and I didn't want to have to be the groom. Aaron and Jenny were going to do it, but the least expensive package was still several hundred dollars.

DAY TRIPS & OVERNIGHT EXCURSIONS

Suzhou

I don't know how to put this diplomatically, or even politely, but I feel strongly that my duty has never been clearer. Forget Suzhou.

I have dreamed of Suzhou; it has been part of my Shanghai fantasies. The Venice of China, a city of canals, home of the old silk factories, pearl-bargain heaven. What's not to like?

Suzhou, now. Maybe Suzhou was great. I don't know when—100 years ago? Fifty years ago? Not last year, trust me.

The silk factories are a joke. The unattractive main shopping street is amusing only in that a) you're a long way from Shanghai architecturally and b) it looks like news footage of Hanoi in 1969. Sure, the pearls are cheap; they're cheap everywhere. You'll have more fun buying pearls in Beijing—I promise.

Getting There: Most people take tours to Suzhou, enjoy its delights as part of their China package, or take a hotel car and driver. You can get there and back by train—it's about an hour-long ride. My hotel concierge quoted a flat fee of $300 for a Mercedes with driver for the day trip. Express buses from the Hong Qiao Airport operate between 10am and 4pm. The bus ride is about an hour and a half.

Shopping Suzhou: Puh-lease.

The Magic City of Zhouzhang

I am reluctant to tell you about this because it is so fabulous that you will rush there immediately and then it will be overrun with tourists and ruined. But because you've just read my rip on Suzhou, and you're thinking I'm as bad as any theater